LEADING & MANAGING INNOVATION

What Every Executive Team Must Know about Project, Program & Portfolio Management

Russell D. Archibald
and
Shane C. Archibald

INFINITY PUBLISHING

ISBN 978-0-7414-8289-1 Paperback
ISBN 978-0-7414-8290-7 eBook
Library of Congress Control Number: 2013901965

Printed in the United States of America

Published February 2013

INFINITY PUBLISHING
1094 New DeHaven Street, Suite 100
West Conshohocken, PA 19428-2713
Toll-free (877) BUY BOOK
Local Phone (610) 941-9999
Fax (610) 941-9959
Info@buybooksontheweb.com
www.buybooksontheweb.com

Praise for *Leading & Managing Innovation*

Dr. Aaron Shenhar:
"This unique book provides a much required integrative view on innovation, project, program, and portfolio management. It should be useful to any executive who is concerned with promoting innovation and execution in the company.

Based on years of experience and writing the authors are conveying a broad understanding of these concepts to executive teams in a concise manner, together with the importance of achieving innovation or major changes within enterprises.

The executive demands listed in Chapter 7 are unique in the project management literature, and if combined with the corporate strategy, can produce excellence in selecting and executing innovative projects."

> Dr. Aaron Shenhar, PMI Fellow, Professor of Management at Stevens Institute of Technology, co-author of Reinventing Project Management: *The Diamond Approach to Successful Growth and Innovation*.

Marc Zocher:
"I believe this book to be much needed, about the correct level for an executive to use/grasp, and timely."

> Marc Zocher, Consultant, as Project Manager received the 2011 PMI Distinguished Project Award for the G2 Information System Project for the U. S. Dept. of Energy's NNSA Global Threat Reduction Initiative.

Wayne Abba:
"This important book explains why executives need to build, support and maintain a mature portfolio management process."

Wayne Abba, Abba Consulting, Internationally known advocate for project and program management using Earned Value, Adviser to the US Government Accountability Office (USGAO)

Bob Prieto:
"In Leading & Managing Innovation Russ and Shane Archibald describe three significant attributes related to successful innovation. First, the importance of the presence or, if necessary, the creation of enabling frameworks is discussed.

Second, the importance of systemic factors to successful innovation is outlined and strategies for capitalizing on the presence of these factors are discussed.

Finally, the case for project driven execution, continuously and acutely focused on well-articulated strategic objectives, is solidly made."

Bob Prieto, Sr. Vice Pres., Flour Corp., author of *Strategic Program Management*.

Paul Dinsmore:
"This book zeroes in on the symbiotic relationship that exists between projects and programs, and the innovations required for organizations to gain market share and prosper.

As the authors point out in this pleasantly formatted and readable book, 'All Significant Innovations are achieved through Projects and Programs.' The special characteristics of innovation are discussed and the book provides an in-depth description of the basics of project management required for insuring that innovation is managed effectively and efficiently.

It will give the reader a solid overview of fundamentals and how those basics can be applied productively in these increasingly challenging times."

> Paul Dinsmore, Dinsmore Associates, PMI Fellow, co-author of *Enterprise Project Governance*, and author of 19 other books on project management.

Dr. Martin Barnes:
"These two really know how to organize and deliver useful new things and useful changes."

> Dr. Martin Barnes OBE; a Founder, Honorary Fellow, and former Chairman and President of the UK Association for Project Management (APM); and former Executive Director of the Major Projects Association (MPA.).

Preface

Innovations don't just happen. To make them real, all significant innovations today are achieved through projects and programs.

Executives in all business, industrial, governmental, and non-governmental organizations need to fully understand the differences between operational and project management principles and practices to best take advantage of the power of good project management and thereby lead and manage the innovation within their enterprise.

This book seeks to satisfy that need by presenting concise descriptions of 1) the key concepts underlying project and program management, 2) the important characteristics of projects and programs, 3) how they are best governed and managed, and 4) how to determine if the desired benefits have actually been achieved.

It also describes what executives can reasonably demand of the project management discipline and of the executives and managers responsible for that discipline within their organizations.

We do not attempt to go into the details here of project planning, estimating, scheduling, reporting and control. A typical description of a project manager's responsibilities for one specific type of project is presented in order to convey the integrative characteristics of that important role in project management.

We hope this book provides executive teams of all shapes and sizes with an increased understanding of what can (and must!) be done to develop, enhance, and support the important innovations within their enterprises. It is only through innovation that significant changes are made and organizations thrive *ahead* of consumer demands. Lead. Follow. Or get out of the way!

Russell D. Archibald

Shane C. Archibald

Acknowledgements

The concepts and ideas presented in this book reflect the experience and knowledge of many people gained over the past six decades. We do not claim to be the originators of these concepts and ideas.

Rather we have tried to observe and describe to the best of our abilities the essence and importance of effective project, program and portfolio management practices in the industrialized world from the executive's viewpoint.

It is not possible to list the names of the hundreds of colleagues, clients, and project management authorities with whom we have worked and learned from over the past 65 years for Russ and 20 years for Shane. We are indebted to all of them and especially to those specific individuals that we have cited in the text for their contributions.

In particular we want to convey our gratitude to Wayne Abba, Dr. Martin Barnes, Paul Dinsmore, Stanislaw Gasik, David Pells, Bob Prieto, Dr. Aaron Shenlar, Miles Shepard, Max Wideman, and Marc Zocher for their useful advice and counsel during the writing and editing of this book.

We wish to acknowledge the dedicated assistance of Barbara Archibald in the preparation of the manuscript of this book.

R. D. A.

S. C. A.

Contents

1
Innovations are Achieved through Projects

Importance of Innovation

Innovation is the process that transforms new ideas into commercial or other value. It is a vital capability in business, entrepreneurship, design, technology of all kinds, health care, engineering, construction, manufacturing, transportation, communications, economics, sociology – and project management.

Innovation is:

- ***Vital*** *to all organizations.*
- ***Accomplished*** *through projects and programs.*

All Executives need to know what is in this book to:

- ***Govern*** *& manage innovation.*
- ***Effectively direct*** *the project management function.*

Innovation means change – something new and improved – in 1) a business or creative *process,* and/or 2) the *output or product of a process.*

Forward looking executives want and encourage their managers to be innovative and to continually improve their processes, products and services.

Innovate or die! In this Digital Age of technological explosion in every field all types of human organizations must continually innovate to improve and change both their products and services (their reason to exist) and also the ways they operate – their business processes.

Continual innovation in both of these dimensions is required for continued success.

Innovate and succeed!

Systemic versus Incremental Innovation

Systemic innovation differs from incremental innovation which can be accomplished within a single firm context or within a discrete project context.

Prieto (2011) points out that "Systemic innovation is that form of innovation that requires 'multiple specialist firms to change their process in a coordinated fashion.'[1]

"Examples of systemic innovation in the engineering and construction industry include:

- Integrated supply chain management.
- Prefabrication of building systems.
- 3D CAD virtual design and construction tools.
- Building Information Models (BIM).
- Project Finance Initiatives (PFI) and Public Private Partnerships (PPP).
- Modularization.

Many of these are characteristic of successful large programs."

Prieto refers to systemic innovation in the largest industry in the world, the engineering construction industry. In the USA this industry accounts for 9% of the GDP.

Systemic innovation is also required in large, multinational companies as well as large governmental agencies.

In smaller organizations systemic innovation can also produce useful results, but it is more likely that incremental innovation is more frequently used in most situations.

---

[1] Taylor, John E. and Raymond Levitt, "Modeling Systemic Innovation in Design and Construction Networks," Center for Integrated Facility Engineering;, CIFE Technical Report # 163. Stanford University, October 2005

Creativity and Innovation

Innovation obviously depends on creative ideas. This book does not explore the sources of new ideas, but rather focuses on how to transform those ideas into desirable benefits.

As Michael Ray and Rochelle Myers state in the introduction to their 1989 book **Creativity in Business:** "One of the main problems in U. S. business today is that there are too many ideas, not too few. Dozens of solutions appear and disappear in chaotic piles of data, crowds of expert opinion, and a jumble of contradictory statistics and reports on every aspect of every issue. The pressure of limited time is increased by indecision and, beneath it all, the nagging suspicion that others will find your efforts insufficient and the results poor."

Innovation Means Change:

- In a business or process.
- In the output or product of the process.

All Significant Innovations are Achieved through Projects

We hope to persuade the reader of this book that this is a valid statement. When that persuasion occurs then it is obvious that all executives in every kind of human enterprise need to know the characteristics of projects and how best to govern and manage projects, programs, and their portfolios.

Some notable characteristics of innovation are:

- The starting point for innovation is the generation of creative ideas. Innovation is the process of taking those ideas to market or to usefulness.

- Innovation concerns the search for and the discovery, experimentation, development, imitation and adoption of new products and services, new processes and new organizational arrangements.

- Innovation is the conversion of knowledge and ideas into a benefit, which may be for commercial use or for the public good; the benefit may be new or improved products, processes or services.
- Innovation is the process that transforms ideas into commercial value.
- Innovation = Invention + Exploitation.

The generally accepted definition of a project is "a temporary endeavor undertaken to create a unique product, service, or result"[2] Programs are "a group of related projects"[3] but in recent years the concept of strategic transformational programs[4] includes both projects and operations (or other activities) within their scope.

A Project is:
A temporary endeavor undertaken to create a unique product, service, or result.

A Program is:
A group of related projects.

A project is the best – perhaps only – method of achieving innovation.

Structured, Well-Managed Innovation

The alternative of simply throwing an idea on the table at a staff meeting and seeing if anyone will start making it happen will not get the job done.

Innovation begins in every case with an idea generated by an individual, or sometimes by a small group of people collaborat-

---

[2] PMIa 2008 p. 442.
[3] Ibid.
[4] See Chapter 2 for further discussion of strategic transformational programs.

ing to solve a problem, develop a new product or service, or create and satisfy a customer need.

Transforming that idea into the reality of something new – a new or improved process, service, or product, or even a new enterprise – is rarely if ever the result of one person's effort, even though one person will lead the effort as the project manager.

This transformation requires a structured approach to bring together all the skills and other resources needed in a structured team and to define the resulting project in terms of its objectives, scope, cost and other resources, and its schedule for completion.

Project Management at the Basic Level:

- Uses a structured approach.
- Brings together all the skills and resources needed.
- Defines the Project in terms of objectives, scope, cost, resources, and schedule.
- Delivers the intended results and value.

This is project management at the basic level.

Steve Jobs, the Computer Mouse, and Innovation through Project Management

Thirty-four years ago Steve Jobs introduced the MacIntosh computer with the mouse. Jobs is a great example of an effective innovator and project manager -- even though he was sometimes described as tyrannical and cruel to many on his staff – and also a genius.

In fact, Jobs was truly Apple's Chief Projects Officer/CPO (discussed in Chapters 2 and 5.)

The transformational innovation of the computer mouse (with several other innovations introduced in the MacIntosh at the same time) was not invented by Jobs, however.

As reported by Gladwell[5] (2011), Engelbart had the mouse idea, which was then developed by Xerox PARC up to a point, and then made practical and marketable by Jobs and Apple Computer with the help of an industrial design firm and a creative team of people within Apple.

The computer mouse development and market introduction exemplifies the need for effective project management when it comes to implementing innovation.

Sometimes Innovation Involves Multiple Parties and Steps:

- Engelbart had the idea.
- Xerox PARC developed the idea.
- Jobs 'finished the job' with the help of an industrial firm and internal design team.

Gladwell's 2011 article in the New Yorker Magazine is titled "Creation Myth – Xerox PARC, Apple, and the Truth about Innovation," and the truth he presents is this: it takes a project with a good project manager to achieve significant innovation.

What All Executives Must Know about Project Management

This book provides the executive reader with a sound understanding of both the characteristics of projects and programs and of the principles to effectively manage them.

It clearly and concisely explains to the executive reader the important differences in:

- **Project management** compared to on-going **operations management**,
- **Transformational** compared to **delivery projects**, and
- **Project-driven** compared to **project-dependent organizations.**

[5] Best-selling author of ***The Tipping Point*** and ***Outliers: the Story of Success.***

Chapter 2 summarizes the basic concepts underlying project and program management.

In Chapter 3 we provide needed understanding about the wide range in the categories and characteristics of projects and programs that exist.

Chapter 4 discusses the capability required to manage projects and programs within portfolios.

Chapter 5 conveys an understanding of the value and need for establishing Project Management Offices (PMOs) as well as the various responsibilities that can be assigned to those offices.

Chapter 6 briefly describes the heart of good project management, namely the methods used to manage each individual project.

Based on the knowledge conveyed in those chapters, Chapter 7 provides executives with a list of what they must demand of their executive and management teams in order to achieve effective project, program, and portfolio management within their enterprises.

Chapters 8 and 9 provide useful background for executives: Chapter 8 discusses achieving and measuring maturity in project management and benchmarking their organization's capabilities in this area against their competitors.

Chapter 9 conveys an understanding of the overall importance today of the discipline of project management around the world. Chapter 10 provides a concise summary of these nine chapters.

Our purpose is to provide executives and senior managers with the information necessary to understand, utilize, and gain a competitive advantage in the process of transforming ideas into real innovation.

"A nation's ability to build and sustain its innovation capacity depends on developing and maintaining project management skills...."
Naughton and Kavanagh, 2009

2
The Essence of the Key Project Management Concepts

This chapter presents the key concepts underlying modern project management principles and practices, and conveys an understanding of their objectives.

The important characteristics of projects are described, and the differences between project-driven and project-dependent organizations are discussed.

A note about terminology: To avoid the repetitious use of "project and program" we will generally use the word "project" in the remainder of this book, since the concepts discussed are applicable to both of these complex efforts.

Where differences are important they will be identified.

Operations and Projects require different management methods.

Integrative roles, systems, and teams are required for project management.

PM must support the organization's approved strategies.

Projects and Programs can be routine or transformational.

Organizations can be project-driven or project-dependent.

Project Management versus Operations Management

All enterprises consist of these two classes of activity:

- ***Operations*** that are ongoing and repetitive, and
- ***Projects and programs*** that are temporary endeavors undertaken to create unique products, services or results, or otherwise significantly change the enterprise.

Project Management vs. Operations Management:
- Operations are ongoing and repetitive.
- Projects are temporary endeavors undertaken to create unique products, services or results.
- Programs sometimes blend projects and operations.

Traditional programs consist of a group of related projects, while ***strategic or transformation programs*** usually include both projects and ongoing operations.

Three Underlying Concepts of Project Management

The three key differentiating characteristics of project management when compared to on-going functional operations management are:

1. Assignment of **integrative responsibilities** for projects and programs at several levels,
2. Application of **integrated project planning and control information systems**, and
3. Execution of the work required for each project by **integrated teams of people** using available, assigned resources.

Each of these three concepts is discussed in the following paragraphs.

Three Key Differences between Projects / Programs & Operations:
- Assignment of Integrative Responsibilities.
- Application of Planning and Control Systems.
- Integrated Teams.

First Concept

Assignment of integrative responsibilities at six levels for project, program and portfolio management:

1. **CEO and other C-level executives** - governmental Ministers, Secretaries, and Senior Executives:
   - Establishing and clearly communicating the enterprise strategies.
   - Assuring the existence of effective program/project management processes.
   - Selecting and prioritizing strategic transformational programs and projects.
   - Allocating available resources to all approved program and project portfolios.

Six levels of Project Management Responsibilities:

1. CEO.
2. Portfolio Steering Group.
3. Executive Project Sponsor.
4. PMO: Project Management Office.
5. Project Managers.
6. Functional Managers.

2. **Portfolio steering groups** (or portfolio governance committees) for their assigned portfolios:
   - Validating that all approved programs and projects support strategic objectives.
   - Prioritizing programs and projects within assigned portfolios and allocating available resources within those portfolios.
   - Overseeing and governing the performance on programs and projects.

3. **Project and program executive sponsors** for assigned major, critical programs and projects: "... project sponsorship is the effective link between the organization's senior executive body and the management of the project. The sponsoring role has decision making, directing and representational accountabilities... Sponsors own the business case. Compe-

tent project sponsorship is of great benefit to even the best project managers."[6]

Their responsibilities include but are not limited to:

- Providing strategic direction to their assigned program or project managers/directors to resolve high level conflicts or make decisions that are beyond those persons' scope of authority, and.
- Monitoring economic and political changes within the environment external to the project or program and reflecting such changes in the strategic direction given to the program or project managers.

4. **Managers of the project management discipline** (Project Management Offices/PMOs or Central Project Offices/CPOs) for their parts of the organization:
   - Developing and improving the program and project management processes, policies, procedures, practices, and tools for their assigned parts of the organization.
   - Providing training of and direction to assigned program and project managers/directors and specialized (project controls) support staff members.
   - Assuring that the best and most appropriate project/program management planning, scheduling, and reporting (project controls) staff assistance and information systems are provided to all project and program managers.
   - Other roles and responsibilities that may be assigned to PMOs within the enterprise (see discussion in Chapter 5).

   Note: The role of Chief Projects Officer (CPO) has emerged in some organizations on a par with other C-

---

[6] APM 2004, Section 4.2.

level executives[7]; this role will usually include responsibility for the corporate PMO.

5. **Project and program managers or directors:**
   - Overall integrative planning, project direction and control of the project through all its phases to achieve the specified results on time and within budget.
   - Building and leading the project team.
   - Evaluating actual progress of the project and exerting their assigned project authority by giving project direction to all functional project team leaders. See further discussion in Chapter 5 below.

6. **Functional (specialist) managers** and their functional project team leaders:
   - Providing the required skilled people, facilities, equipment and other resources and giving them integrative, functional direction, in compliance with the project/program direction from the project/program manager regarding the specified scope of results, quality, schedule, and budget for their assigned functional work.
   - Actively participating in project and program planning, scheduling, monitoring, and reporting activities in compliance with the enterprise's established project management processes and procedures.

These roles and responsibilities are fully described in the abundant, current project management literature (for example see Archibald 2003, pp 82-106 and 201-225). For the project and functional managers the key aspects of these responsibilities relating to their assigned project tasks within individual projects are discussed in more detail in Chapter 6.

---

[7] PMI PM Network, Dec. 2010, pp. 30-31.

Project Stakeholders: In addition to the above direct responsibilities it is important to recognize that the stakeholders in any project or program also include all persons or agencies that are affected by or exert influence over the conduct of or the results from the project.

Project Stakeholders:
- Must be identified early.
- Their satisfaction determines how successful the project will be.

Project success often depends as much on inside and outside stakeholders as it does on those directly responsible for the effort.

Regulating authorities are obviously important stakeholders in many projects and programs.

Second Concept
Application of integrative and predictive practices, processes, methods, information systems and related tools (project controls):

These produce and effectively use the information required to plan, schedule, monitor, report, and control the scope, risks, schedules, resources and costs of projects, programs and project portfolios, while integrating their entire project life cycles.

Historically these were most often based on once-through, deterministic methods, although iterative, heuristic, and "agile" processes are now often used or required, mainly for software or R&D projects -- but these iterative processes still have a predictive and control objective for the entire project.

Project Controls Systems:
Computer-based information systems today are advanced and powerful and require well-trained staff to be effective.

A large number of computer-supported, Internet-enabled information systems are presently available to assist with these planning, scheduling, reporting, and controlling tasks, ranging from simple, single-project applications to enterprise-wide information systems. See further discussion in Chapters 4 and 6.

Third Concept
Assigning, building and directing each project team:

The nature of the project obviously determines the skilled people and other resources that will be required to plan and execute the project.

Selection and assignment of the project team members is usually a negotiation process involving the Project Executive Sponsor, functional (line) managers, and the project manager.

A primary responsibility of each assigned project and program manager is to build a cohesive team that is comprised of the multi-disciplined functional managers and specialists (project team leaders), plus the project controls specialists, needed to plan, schedule, estimate, execute, and manage each project and program.

This is a delicate and important task; often team members arrive from previous projects bringing their strong opinions about what worked or didn't work on the last one.

> **A primary responsibility of the Project/Program Manager is to build and lead a cohesive multi-disciplinary team.**
>
> - The nature of the project determines the resources and skills required
> - Selection of the team members is usually a negotiation process
> - The Project/Program Manager leads the team either directly or through the functional managers or both.

This team building exercise must consider the opinions of the new members and the artifacts carried forward but must immediately establish the framework for how this program or project will work to achieve the desired cohesion.

The project manager leads the team and gives project direction to all team members, usually through the functional managers who are providing the needed skilled people.

Project direction uses the integrative project information systems mentioned earlier and focuses primarily on **what** work has to be done (project scope), **when** it must be completed, and **how much** labor and other costs are available in the project budget for its completion. Ideally the project scope, budget and schedule are established with agreement between the project manager and the functional managers supporting the project.

Functional vs. Program or Project Direction:

- **Project/Program direction** is usually given by the Project/Program Manager
- **Functional direction** is usually given by the functional manager.

Functional direction is given to the functional project team members by the assigned functional manager. This direction consists of **how** the work is to be done; **what quality** and other specifications are to be met to achieve the project objectives, including its scope, schedule, budget, and quality of the results produced; and **who** will be assigned to actually do the work.

A project is not really a live project until the project team is assembled and begins their work to plan and execute the many tasks that must be completed to achieve the project objectives.

The primary role of the project manager is to lead and motivate the project team throughout the life of the project.

These three basic concepts underlie all of the policies, principles, and practices of project management.

In almost every case the evolution of the program and project management discipline within a complex organization results in a project/functional matrix of responsibilities that can range from a weak to a strong matrix, referring to the authority of the project and program managers to give project direction to the project and program team members that are doing the work.

If a project or program manager tries to give functional direction to project team members, even when he or she is very skilled in that particular function, without the complete involvement and agreement of the responsible functional manager, serious conflict will result.

The Objectives of Project Management Are Two-Fold

1. To assure that each project and program, when initially conceived and authorized, **supports the organization's approved higher level strategic objectives** and contains acceptable risks regarding the project's or program's objectives: political, competitive, technical, cost and schedule.
2. To plan, schedule, control and lead each authorized project -- simultaneously with all other projects and programs within the enterprise -- effectively and efficiently so that **each will achieve its approved objectives:** meeting its related strategic objective by producing the specified results on schedule and within budget, with satisfaction for all affected stakeholders.

The first of these over-arching objectives is closely linked to the strategic management of the organization.

Application of project management practices during the early strategic planning and project concept phases has been introduced in more organizations within the past years with beneficial results.

The Objectives of Project & Program Management are Two-Fold:

- To ensure each project or program supports the organization's strategies and contains acceptable risks
- To plan, schedule, control, and lead each project effectively and efficiently and effectively.

Too frequently, project failures can be traced directly to unrealistic original technical, cost or schedule targets, and inadequate risk analysis and risk management.

It should be emphasized that if the right projects are not selected in the first place, even an enterprise with the best project management planning, scheduling, and execution maturity will not be successful. Planning and executing the wrong projects that do not achieve the enterprise's strategic objectives can be as risky as the right projects managed poorly.

Strategic Transformative versus Traditional or Routine Projects

It is necessary and useful to recognize the differences between:

- **Major, strategic transformative projects** that are intended to change or transform the enterprise significantly and thereby achieve its strategic vision, mission and objectives, and
- **Routine "delivery", "commercial", "deployment", "process, service, or product improvement", or "compliance" projects** that generate income and profit, reduce cost, otherwise improve the services or products provided to the enterprise's customers or constituents, or comply with laws and regulations, within the enterprise's established strategic vision and objectives, without creating significant changes within the enterprise itself.

Strategic Transformative versus Traditional or Routine:

- Transformative Projects and Programs are those intended to change or transform the enterprise significantly.
- Routine Projects and Programs are those intended to provide a product or service that may generate income or provide compliance with laws or stakeholder requirements and expectations; they do not significantly change the organization.

Table 2.1. Basic Differences of Project Types.
Source: Pfeiffer 2004, p 5.

Basic Differences of Project Types	
Deployment [Delivery] Project	**Development [Transformational] Project**
Civil construction. Installation of a system.	Development of new products. Organization of social change.
Advance measured by products. "Final Product" relatively clear.	Advance aimed at reducing uncertainties, measured by indicators.
Life Cycle generally cascade.	Various life cycles possible.
Leadership style based on command and control.	Leadership style focused on learning.
Highly structured information system.	Less formal communication system.
Task oriented organization of Human Resources.	Human Resources need to adapt and evolve in order to respond to changes.
Progress relatively linear.	Processes very dynamic.

Pfeiffer (2004) describes a useful approach to differentiating between what he calls "deployment" and "development" projects. Table 2.1 shows his comparison of these two project types.

Strategic Transformative Programs

While the traditional definition of a program as "consisting of a group of related projects" is widely used in many industries and governmental agencies, in recent years most authorities observe that program management has evolved in many organizations to encompass a broader range of activities with broader objectives.

Traditional Program:
A group of related projects.

Strategic Transformative Program:
Projects and other actions that form an enterprise within the enterprise.

Thiry (2010, p.16) defines program management as ***"The governance and harmonized management of a number of projects and other actions to achieve stated business benefits and create value for the stakeholders."***

We prefer to differentiate this from the traditional definition by using Thiry's definition to refer to ***strategic transformative programs***. The "other actions" in his definition are typically operational in nature within the enterprise, and the broader objectives "**to achieve stated business benefits and create value for the stakeholders**" are predominantly strategic in nature.

This valid, new definition shows us that a strategic transformative program is truly ***an enterprise within the parent enterprise***, whereas a typical project, with its limited scope, time, and well-defined objectives and deliverables, is just that: a project.

There can of course be large, major projects (in addition to strategic programs) that are truly strategic and transformational in nature.

Several projects do not usually make a strategic program, in this latest understanding of what an enterprise-changing program is.

Project-Driven versus Project-Dependent Enterprises

Project-driven enterprises, such as those in facilities design and construction, consulting companies, aerospace and defense contractors, information technology system suppliers, and other enterprises for whom projects are the primary source of their revenue, may be very mature in the management of these delivery projects, but much less mature in managing transformative programs and projects that introduce major changes within their enterprises.

Project-dependent enterprises, including most governmental agencies in the world (except those few like NASA and some governmental transportation departments, as examples, that are project-driven), manufacturers and businesses selling established products and services, banks and financial services, and many others, derive most of their revenue from selling products or services, or delivering benefits to their customers or constituents (as for most governmental and non-governmental organizations), and not from selling projects that create and deliver new products and services.

Project Driven vs. Project Dependent Organizations:

Project-Driven Organizations:
- Rely on projects for normal revenue.
- Are usually mature in the management of these "delivery" projects.
- May be less mature in management of transformative programs and projects.

Project-Dependent Organizations:
- Derive most of their revenues from selling products or services.
- Rely on projects and project management for expansion or development of new products or processes.
- Often employ Project-Driven organizations for specific needs.

Projects, however, are vital to their continued growth and prosperity: to develop new products or services, enter new markets, expand their facilities, and so on.

Strategic transformational programs and major projects within these project-dependent enterprises often include the purchase under contract of delivery projects from project-driven enterprises.

Origins of Projects: The Incubation/Feasibility Phase[8]

In almost every case the standard "Project Starting Phase" must begin with a reasonable understanding of what the principle objectives, scope, desired schedule, and order of magnitude cost of the project are expected to be, including:

- What the project will create (new product, facility, service, information system, organization, other principle deliverables).

- What business benefits will be produced for the organization that will pay for the project, as will be detailed in the Business Case that is produced during the Project Starting Phase.

- Verification that the project is aligned with the strategic plans and objectives of the sponsoring organization.

- A reasonable idea of the overall scope of the project together with its expected time schedule and cost, and whether the needed money and other key resources can reasonably be expected to be available, as will be verified and detailed in the Project Charter that is produced during the Project Starting Phase.

- Preliminary or conditional approvals that the project will require from governmental authorities or other agencies (environmental, economic, health, others) as well as any intellectual property and physical rights of access that are needed for the project to succeed.

---

[8] R. Archibald, I. DiFilippo, D. DiFilippo, "The Six Phase Comprehensive Project Life Cycle Model Includes the Project Incubation/Feasibility Phase and the Project Post-Completion Phase," 2012.

- Overall economic, technological, political, social[9], and physical feasibility of the project, including the level and acceptability of the various risks that are involved.

A project will not normally be authorized to enter the Project Starting Phase until sufficient information, as listed above, is available and its feasibility has been established.

The basic question here is: **"Where does this initial 'embryonic knowledge and understanding' about the potential project come from?"**

This information must be accumulated through a process of "information buffering[10]" (Di Filippo 2011) over a period of time prior to authorizing any project to enter the current standard Project Starting Phase, and this occurs in every case during the usually undefined but always present **Project Incubation/Feasibility Phase**.

This information buffering is similar to downloading a movie on your television set: the movie (or the project) cannot begin until sufficient data and knowledge has been obtained and compiled locally.

Project versus Strategic Management

Projects originate to support the strategic goals of the enterprise.

The project management discipline must be correlated with the strategic management discipline.

Table 2.2 indicates the usual sources of the "embryonic knowledge and understanding" of these two types of projects within the two organizational types described above.

---

[9] For example, the social feasibility of designing and constructing a nuclear power plant in 2013 near Fukishimo, Japan, is considered to be close to zero.

[10] We "buffer" and store in an appropriate manner the information about the project, its scope, results and feasibility, and the cognitive constraints that exist within the project team members.

Table 2.2.
Origins of two project types within project-driven and project-dependent organizations.

Project Type → Organization Type:	Commercial or Delivery Projects	Development or Transformational Projects
Project-Driven Organizations	*** Marketing or Business Development Department develops four project portfolios:** 1) customer relationship, 2) network relationship, delivery, and 3) offering portfolios.[11] They evaluate requests for proposals-RFPs from customers that result from usually long-lasting relationships and extensive marketing efforts, or develop proposals initiated internally. *** Project proposals that comply** with well-established strategic goals and are within the known capabilities of the organization are prepared and approved prior to sub-	***Statements below for Project-Dependent Organizations also apply here to Project-Driven Organizations.**

[11] Tikkanen et al 2007.

	mittal to the customers. ***Project Starting Phase** is not initiated until a proposal is negotiated and a contract is signed by both parties. ***A full-time Project Manager** is usually appointed only during the Project Starting Phase. * **Project management functions** must be applied in proposal preparation but frequently they are not.	
Project-Dependent Organizations	* **Few if any** commercial/delivery projects exist in these organizations. If so the above comments apply.	***Ideas for projects** for major organizational change; acquisitions; mergers; or new markets, products, processes or services **come from** strategic managers, marketing/business development, R&D, past customers, consultants, or individuals.

		***Development of the idea** into **project objectives, scope, et al** occurs over a period of time prior to the project entering the Starting Phase. * Only when **the 'embryonic understanding' of the potential project** has been approved does the project enter the Project Starting Phase.

It is worth noting that many transformational projects or programs include the purchase of delivery projects from outside suppliers that are actually project-driven companies or agencies.

This depends on the internal decision whether to "buy" or to "make" the products or results for selected portions (subprojects) of the transformational project or program.

Post-Project Evaluation Phase

Following the current standard Project Close-Out Phase, the Post-Project Evaluation Phase is required to first determining and also maintaining, improving, and even perfecting the ultimate success of:

1) The project from a project management viewpoint.
2) The project's products and results.
3) All project stakeholders' perspectives of both the project and its results, including turnover of people both during the project and after the Project Closeout Phase,

and subsequent application of lessons learned for use on future projects.

4) The overall project and its products from the cognitive constraint perspective.

Evaluation of project success and value is discussed in more detail in Chapter 6.

Since project and program management obviously deals with the type of human effort that we call projects and programs, it is very important that executives everywhere have a good **understanding of what projects are and the broad range of the results that they produce.**

The following chapter is intended to satisfy that need.

3
Categories and Characteristics of Projects

Here we describe the need for systematically categorizing the many different types of projects that exist, discuss a few of the many possible ways to categorize them, and present a widely used project categorization approach that has proven practical for many organizations[12].

Projects and programs in different categories *exhibit very different characteristics and life cycles, and require different management approaches.*

A systematic method *for categorizing projects & programs is required.*

12 proven project categories *are discussed in this chapter.*

The Need for Categorizing Projects and Programs

Significant differences exist between the many projects within:

- The total spectrum of actual projects that exist in the worlds of government, business and industry, and
- The smaller numbers of different kinds of projects that are being planned and executed within one organizational entity or enterprise.

---

[12] Archibald, Russell D., "A Global Systems for Categorizing Projects," **IPMA Project Perspectives 2013.**

Practical experience over many decades in creating and managing the many types (or categories) of projects that exist has led to:

One-size or standard of project management does not fit all projects.

- Recognition that the diversity inherent within the many existing and potential projects demands that projects be segregated in several ways for several purposes, to continue to improve the ways in which both the buyers (owners) and sellers (contractors or developers) manage specific projects.
- Recognition, definition and understanding of the project management (PM) principles and practices ***common to all (or at least many) projects*** in all types of human endeavors and organizations, as documented in the several PM bodies of knowledge and the PM literature in general.

Project Management Principles & practices are common across project categories.

These categorization purposes are to:

- Strategically and operationally select, authorize, and prioritize their projects.
- Operationally plan and execute their projects:
    - individually,
    - within programs, and
    - within project portfolios.
- Educate and train the managers and specialists involved in projects and PM.
- Develop and manage the careers of managers and specialists involved in creating and managing projects, the project management discipline, and its informational tools.

Methods of Project Categorization

A number of project attributes that can be used to categorize or classify projects have been identified by Crawford et al (2005), but to date there is not one method or system in use across all industries or governments. Of the many possibilities we present four different approaches here that convey some of the important characteristics of projects and programs.

Methods of Project Categorization

- Size, Complexity and Familiarity
- Life Cycle or Sector
- Contract Type and Payment Terms
- Observation of de-facto project categorization
- More...

De facto project categorization or specialization: Today, within the PM practices of large and small organizations and within some of the recognized PM bodies of knowledge and standards, we can see *de facto* categorization of projects for various purposes.

Many PM practitioners report that "our organization does not categorize our projects in any formal way." However, the structure of their organization itself usually creates *de facto* categorization.

De Facto categorization of projects exists in most organizations.

For example, it is common for one company, or one division/department of a larger company, to be devoted only to IT hardware (new product development) and/or software projects, which are in themselves important project categories.

The larger facilities engineering/construction companies often create operating divisions devoted to sub-categories of projects such as energy plants, commercial structures, high-rise buildings, dams, and transportation (highways, bridges, etc.). Many companies or government agencies are devoted to only one or a few categories of projects.

Movement toward broader recognition that one PM standard does not fit all projects is demonstrated by the production of various standards in recent years within both the Project Management Institute /PMI® and some of the more than 50 national associations that are members of the International Project Management Association/IPMA, as discussed further in Chapter 9.

For example, the top five areas of PM application/industries represented by the 395,965 members (as of December 2012) of PMI in 120 countries are "computers/software/data processing, information technology, telecommunications, business management, and financial services" (*PMI Corporate Council Update* March 2003, p 3, the latest published data available for these categories), even though the facilities construction and aerospace/defense industries are the most mature PM areas of application in most countries.

A systematic approach to project categorization is necessary to achieve the most effective PM success and to accelerate the development of and improvements in the PM discipline.

A systematic approach to project categorization delivers measurable improvements.

Research (see Crawford et al 2005 and Archibald 2007) shows that there are many characteristics and attributes of projects that can be used, and in fact are being used, to categorize and/or classify projects. There are also many purposes and uses of the various categorizations.

Strategic categorization by market share & strategic intent

One method (Fern 2004) for categorizing projects according to market share and strategic intent combines the Boston Consulting Group's well-known matrix (Figure 3.1, relating product or service market share with market growth) and Hammel and Prahalad's (1989) theory that products are developed to conform to the requirements of one of three strategic intents: technological excellence, operational excellence, or customer intimacy.

This method of project categorization is useful when allocating limited resources and prioritizing projects that are competing for those common resources, including funding, skilled people, and specialized facilities and equipment.

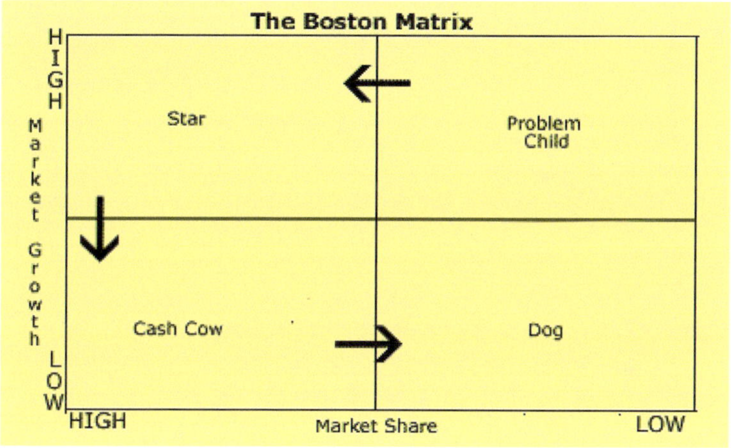

Figure 3.1. The Boston Matrix.

Project categorization by scope and technology

Shenhar et al (1996) provide an excellent examination and discussion of attributes that can be used to classify projects from the perspective of relationships between project scope and technology content and uncertainty, as shown in Fig. 3.2.

Categorizing projects in this manner can be useful to determine the qualifications and assigned authority of the project (or program) manager or director, and also the specific project management tools and processes to be used to plan, estimate, assess and manage risks, evaluate, report and control the project.

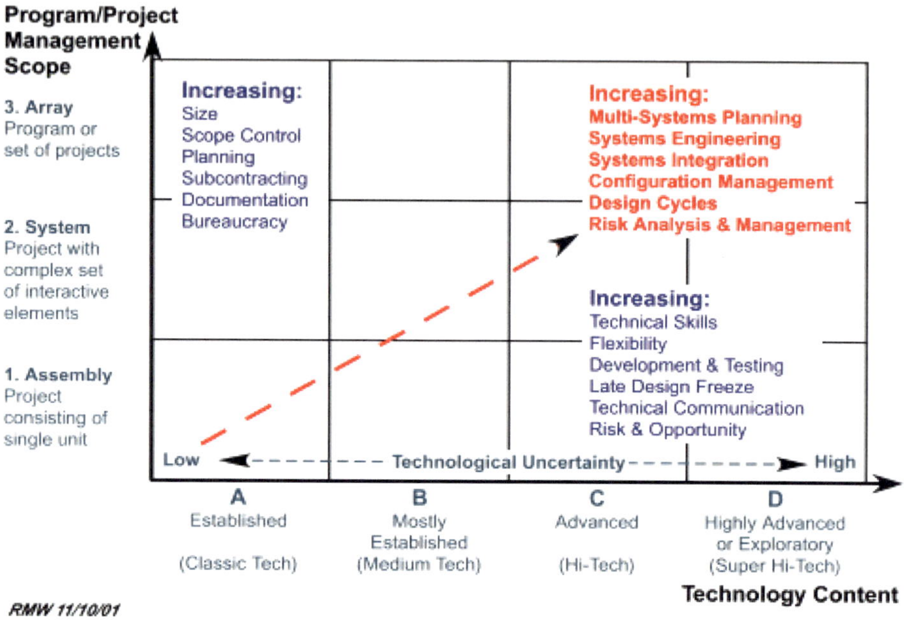

Figure 3.2. Relationships between Project Scope and Technology Content and Uncertainty.
Source: Shenhar et al, 1996. Used with permission.

The Project Diamond Model to Distinguish Between Projects

Shenhar (2012) and Shenhar and Dvir (2007) have developed an innovative and useful approach to distinguishing between projects with their Project Diamond Model. This model enables a project to be rated on four axes: complexity, technology, novelty, and pace.

Figure 3.3 shows the four attributes that are used in this model to indicate where a specific project falls on each of these.

Figure 3.4 provides more details used to place a specific project on each axis.

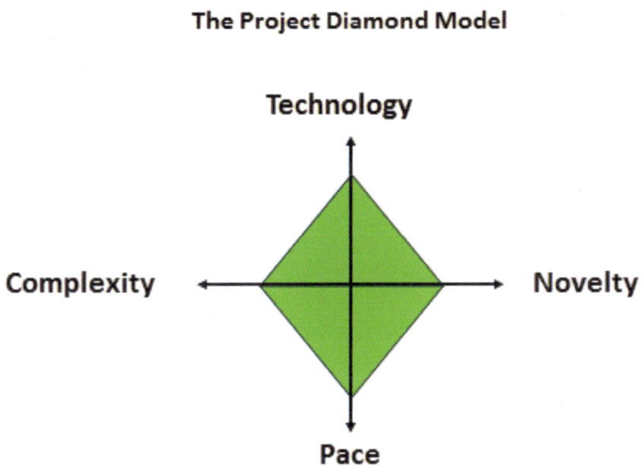

Figure 3.3. Using the Project Diamond Model to Distinguish Between Projects. Source: Shenhar 2012. Used with permission.

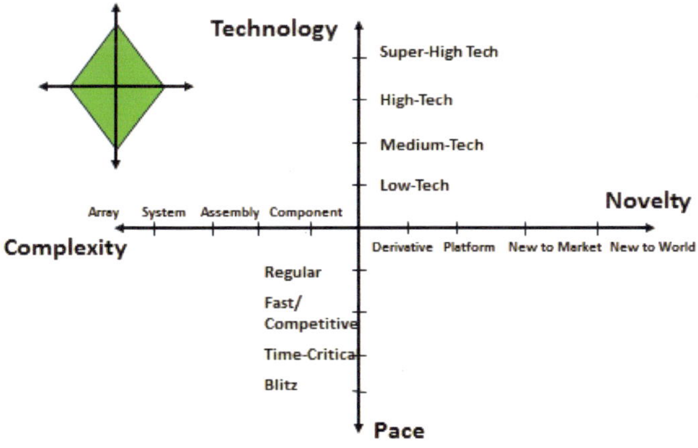

Figure 3.4. Project Types within the Project Diamond Model
Source: Shenhar 2012. Used with permission.

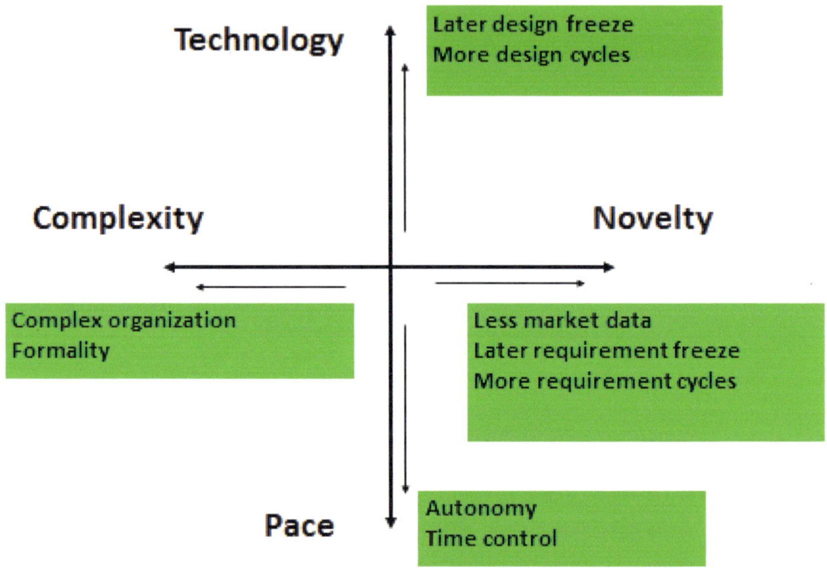

Figure 3.5. The Impact of the Diamond Dimensions on Project Management.
Source: Shenhar 2012. Used with permission.

Figure 3.5 illustrates the impact of these dimensions on the project management methods required for the project in question. Armed with this knowledge responsible executives can determine the best approach to governing and managing the project.

Categorizing by a Project's Products and/or Other Results

From the perspectives of achieving project success and of developing and improving project management capabilities within an enterprise, categorizing projects by end product or results has proven to be useful, because the type of product or service determines the type of work involved and hence the best methodologies for managing the project.

The basic premise is simple: for a project to be successful, different types of project work associated with different types of product need to be managed differently. An experienced engineering-procurement-construction (EPC) project manager will often not be very successful managing a typical information technology (IT) software project. The project management methods and tools that are successful for an EPC facilities project are not very useful for an IT or new product development project.

A proven categorization method based primarily on the project end results is shown in Table 3.1. Sub-categories are shown for several of the twelve major project categories.

For a discussion of the very distinctive project lifecycle models that are used for the various categories in this table see Archibald 2003, pp. 40-49.

Concerning the important Category 5 Facilities, shown in Table 3.1, even though the design, procurement, construction, and commissioning phases of these projects (which are often called "capital" projects or capital investments) must all be integrated for effective project management, the design and construction phases are often treated as separate project categories when one company performs the engineering design phase and another company carries out the procurement, construction and commissioning phases.

Table 3.1.
Project categories/sub-categories with each category having similar project life cycle phases and project management process.
Source: Archibald 2013, p 9.

Project Categories: with similar life cycle project management models/processes	**Examples**
1. Aerospace/Defense Projects 1.1 Defense systems 1.2 Space 1.3 Military operations	New weapon system; major system upgrade. Satellite development/launch; space station modification. Task force invasion.
2. Business & Organization Change Projects 2.1 Acquisition/Merger 2.2 Management process improvement 2.3 New business venture 2.4 Organization restructuring 2.5 Legal proceeding	Acquire and integrate competing company. Major improvement in project management. Form and launch new company. Consolidate divisions and downsize company. Major litigation case.
3. Communication Systems Projects 3.1 Network communications systems 3.2 Switching communications systems	Microwave communications network. 4th generation wireless communication system.
4. Event Projects 4.1 International events 4.2 National events	2012 Summer Olympic Games; 2014 World Cup Match. 2013 U. S. Super Bowl; 2016 U. S. Political Conventions.
5. Facilities Projects 5.1 Facility decommissioning 5.2 Facility demolition 5.3 Facility maintenance and modification 5.4 Facility design-procurement-construction Civil Energy Environmental High-rise Industrial Commercial Residential Ships	Closure of nuclear power station. Demolition of high rise building. Process plant maintenance turnaround. Conversion of plant for new products/markets. Dam; highway interchange. Power generation plant; pipeline. Chemical waste cleanup. 40 story office building. New manufacturing plant. Shopping center; office building. New housing sub-division. Tanker, container, or passenger ship.
6. Information Systems (Software) Projects	New project management information system. (Information system hardware is in the product development category.)

7. International Development Projects 7.1 Agriculture/rural development 7.2 Education 7.3 Health 7.4 Nutrition 7.5 Population 7.6 Small-scale enterprise 7.7 Infrastructure: energy (oil, gas, coal, power generation and distribution), industrial, telecommunications, transportation, urbanization, water supply and sewage, irrigation)	People and process intensive projects in developing countries funded by The World Bank, regional development banks, US AID, UNIDO, other UN, and government agencies; and Capital/civil works intensive projects—often somewhat different from *5. Facility Projects* as they may include, as part of the project, creating an organizational entity to operate and maintain the facility, and lending agencies impose their project life cycle and reporting requirements.
8. Media & Entertainment Projects 8.1 Motion picture 8.2 TV segment 8.3 Live play or music event	New motion picture. New TV episode. New opera premiere.
9. Product and Service Development Projects 9.1 Information tech. Hardware 9.2 Industrial product/process 9.3 Consumer product/process 9.4 Pharmaceutical product/process 9.5 Service (financial, other)	New desk-top computer. New earth-moving machine. New automobile, new food product. New cholesterol-lowering drug. New life insurance/annuity offering.
10. Research and Development Projects 10.1 Environmental 10.2 Industrial 10.3 Economic development 10.4 Medical 10.5 Scientific	Measure changes in the ozone layer. How to reduce pollutant emission. Determine best crop for sub-Sahara Africa. Test new breast cancer treatment. Determine if life exists on Mars.
11. Healthcare Projects	Major surgical procedure.
12. Other Categories?	Disaster recovery, other…

Classifying projects within categories and sub-categories: There is usually a wide range in the size, risk and complexity of projects within each project category or sub-category in large organizations. The project management process for each project category must provide the flexibility to choose the proper level of planning and control for large, complex, high-risk, 'new territory' projects compared to smaller or 'old hat' projects. Therefore it is desirable to further classify projects within categories or sub-categories using some of the attributes identified by Crawford et al (2005), or using some of the following classifying characteristics.

Classifying Projects within Categories & Sub-Categories:

- **Major or Minor Projects**
  Size (money, scope, duration, etc.); relative to organizational size and experience
- **Project Complexity & Risk**
  Number of different skills or technologies needed, geography/cultures/languages; risks can be financial, technological, political, time pressure, or others
- **Strategic Transformational**
  Multiple projects (and programs) that also directly involve on-going operations
- **Mega Projects and Programs**
  Major projects on steroids, usually major programs over a number of years

Major and Minor Projects within a Category

It is useful to identify at least two classes of projects within each category. Some organizations use three or even four classes within a specific category. For purposes of discussion here we will call these major and minor projects, although each organization can probably define more descriptive names for their situation. The distinction between these major and minor classes will be noted in the following definitions.

Major Projects are those whose large size, great complexity and/or higher risks require:

- Designation of an Executive Project Sponsor;
- Assignment of a full-time Project (or Program) Manager or Director;
- The full application of the complete project management process specified for the particular project catego-

ry for major projects (all specified forms, approvals, plans, schedules, budgets, controls, reports, frequent project review meetings, with substantial levels of detail in each.)

Minor Projects are those whose size, simplicity and low risk allow:

- No formal assignment of an Executive Project Sponsor; sponsor role retained within the line organization.
- One project manager to manage two or more minor projects simultaneously;
- Less than the full application of the complete project management process for the project category (selected basic forms, approvals, plans, schedules, budgets, controls, reports, less frequent project review meetings, with less detail required in each.)

Project Complexity and Risk

The complexity of a project is indicated by the:

- Diversity inherent in the project objectives and scope.
- Number of different internal and external organizations involved, which is usually an indication of the number of required specialized skills.
- Sources and complexity of technology required.
- Sources of funding.
- External or internal customer.
- Degree of customer Involvement in the project.
- Levels of risk (economic, technical, political, other).

Strategic Transformational Projects and Programs

As discussed earlier in Chapter 2, these innovative projects and programs will obviously be major, complex, and usually high risk endeavors to which the above considerations will apply.

"Mega" Projects and Programs

Beyond the preceding discussion of programs and projects within an enterprise there is a special class of human endeavors that have been given the name "Mega."

These usually involve both governmental and private enterprises, and typically involve consortiums of large companies. Examples include the Channel Tunnel railroad from London to Calais; each of today's International Olympic Games events; the design, construction, and commissioning of large industrial complexes with residential cities in previously uninhabited areas of the world; and recovery from large, natural disasters.

Such enormous undertakings, which can last up to 15 to 20 years in some cases, present unique governance and management challenges and are beyond the scope of this present book.

For an authoritative and useful presentation on this subject we recommend the book **Strategic Program Management** (Prieto 2008.)

The Major Projects Association was formed in the United Kingdom in 1981 to address the challenges posed by mega projects and programs.

"The purpose of the Major Projects Association is to improve the initiation and delivery of major projects through the interaction of members from all sectors in sharing experience, knowledge and ideas," according to Dr. Martin Barnes CBE, Former Executive Director, Major Projects Association. See www.majorprojects.org for more information.

"Innovation has to be regarded as an investment, and the way it is measured is different than traditional avenues of investment.

Innovation projects must be evaluated differently than other types of projects, and organizations must learn to manage innovation in parallel to the mainline business using the right procedures & KPIs.

Most innovative projects will be killed very quickly if evaluated using the same parameters as regular projects."

Ahi Gvirtsman, HP Software's head of innovation.

With this understanding of the wide range of project and program categories, sizes, importance, complexity, and end results, we turn our attention in the following chapter to **how these can best be governed and managed within appropriate portfolios.**

4
Project Portfolio Management

"Portfolio management allows organizations to apply real world constraints – such as human and financial resources and their tolerance for risk – and identify those investments that will return the highest strategic value given the current situation, be they projects, programmes or other initiatives" - Butler (2010).

As enterprises mature in the project management discipline they recognize that projects, like all investments, must be managed on a portfolio basis.

Program management is a step in the right direction, but more formalized project portfolio management goes beyond traditional program management.

The key differences between portfolio and multiple project management are shown in Table 4.1.

Projects & Programs *must be managed within portfolios for the most effective use of resources.*

Governance *of these portfolios is a strategic job.*

Integrated information *and prioritization are the major challenges in portfolio management.*

Major benefits *and strategic gains are reported from good project-program portfolio management practices.*

A Program or Project Portfolio is a group of programs or projects related to a well-defined strategic objective.

Table 4.1.
High-Level Comparison of Project Portfolio Management and Multiple Project Management
(Source: Dye and Pennypacker, 2000).

	Project Portfolio Management	**Multiple Project Management**
Purpose	Project Selection and Prioritization	Resource Allocation
Focus	Strategic	Tactical
Planning Emphasis	Long & Medium-Term (annual/quarterly)	Short-Term (day-to-day)
Responsibility	Executive/Senior Management	Project/Resource Managers

Types of Project Portfolios

Within a small enterprise there may be only one overall corporate project portfolio, but it generally makes more sense to define more than one portfolio on a strategic basis in large organizations to reflect product line, geographic or technological divisions of the organization, industry or market.

Portfolio Management
(vs. Project or Program Management)

- Is strategic in nature.
- Goes beyond traditional project or program management.
- Allows organizations to apply real world constraints and risks.
- Provides major benefits and strategic gains.

In these larger organizations portfolios are defined and identified in several ways.

In general a project portfolio is a group of several "delivery" or "commercial" projects that are related to a well-defined major strategic objective, as illustrated in Fig. 4.1.

Strategic transformative projects and programs may be managed within a portfolio or as stand-alone efforts, depending on their size and complexities.

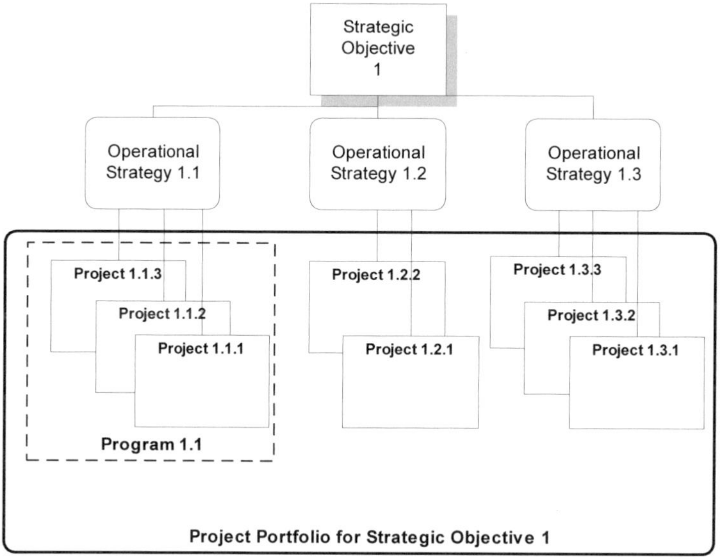

Figure 4.1. Schematic of Strategies, Projects, a Program and a Project Portfolio
Source: Archibald 2003, p 13.

Portfolios are usually named to indicate the nature of the strategic objectives they are meant to achieve. Generic examples include (from Combe and Givens 1999):

- Value-creating: New or improved product, service, or market
- Operational process improvement: Projects that make the organization more efficient and satisfy some fundamental functional work.
- Compliance: "Must-do" projects required to maintain regulatory compliance.

Others have defined other types of project portfolios that reflect the that reflect the specific organizational and industrial environments that are involved.[13]

Three Types of Innovation Investments

According to Harvard Professor Clayton M. Christensen[14], "Executives and investors might finance three types of innovations with their capital," and he goes on to identify these three portfolio types:

- **"Empowering" innovations** that "create jobs, because they require more and more people who can build, distribute, sell and service these products. Empowering investments also use capital – to expand capacity and to finance receivables and inventory."

- **"Sustaining" innovations** that "replace old products with new models.... They keep our economy vibrant — and, in dollars, they account for the most innovation. But they have a neutral effect on economic activity and on capital."

- **"Efficiency" innovations** that "reduce the cost of making and distributing existing products and services.... Taken together in an industry, such innovations almost always reduce the net number of jobs, because they streamline processes. But they also preserve many of the remaining jobs — because without them entire companies and industries would disappear in competition against companies abroad that have innovated more efficiently."

---

[13] Pellegrinelli 1997; Dye and Pennypacker 1999; United Kingdom Government, **Best Management Portfolio: Management of Portfolios 2002**; **PMI The Standard for Portfolio Management** 2008.
[14] "A Capitalist's Dilemma, Whoever Wins on Tuesday," The New York Times, Nov. 3, 2012.

However an enterprise defines their innovative project portfolios they must establish an effective process for managing these portfolios.

Project Portfolio Management Process

A typical project portfolio management process consists of these 12 steps (not always in this identical sequence):

1. Define the project portfolios required.
2. Define the project categories that will exist within each portfolio based on uniform criteria.
3. Identify and group all current and proposed projects within appropriate categories and programs.
4. Validate all projects with the organization's strategic objectives.
5. Prioritize projects within programs and portfolios.
6. Develop each project portfolio master schedule.
7. Establish and maintain a key resources data bank.
8. Allocate available resources to programs and projects within each portfolio.
9. Compare financial needs (primarily cash flow) with availability.
10. Decide how to respond to shortfalls in money or other key resources and approve list of funded projects and their priorities.
11. Plan, authorize, and manage each program and project and its risks using the organization's PM process and supporting systems and tools for each project category. *This step comprises the entire practice of what has traditionally been thought of as "project management."*
12. Periodically reprioritize, reallocate resources to, and reschedule all programs and projects as required within each portfolio (Archibald 2003, pp 12-14 and 175-177).

A coherent, documented Project Portfolio Management Process and a Portfolio Steering Group are vital requirements in today's globally competitive environment.

In organizations that are mature in their PM capabilities a *Project Portfolio Steering Group* (or *Portfolio Governance Committee)* is responsible for this process and for making the decisions that are involved in its effective use, with support from the appropriate Project Management Office/PMO.

The Power of Portfolio Management

The Project Management Institute/PMI reported (PMI 2012) these conclusions from a survey of 443 global portfolio managers:

"Project portfolio management can be a potent weapon to ensure an organization's investments work together and deliver true business results."

- "Project portfolio management can be a potent weapon to ensure an organization's investments work together and deliver true business results.

  Organizations with little variation in their project portfolio management practices see 64% of their projects meet expected ROI—17 percentage points more than those companies with high variability."

"The number of projects completed on time and on budget would increase by roughly one-third with more effective portfolio management."

- "The study also reveals potential for even more significant gains: The 443 global portfolio managers surveyed said **the number of projects completed on time and on budget would increase by roughly one-third with more effective portfolio management.** They also thought achieving objectives and ROI goals would see similar gains."

Published Guides and Standards for Project Portfolio Management

The several professional associations devoted to project and program management (see Chapter 9) and also several government agencies have produced a number of guides and standards for various aspects of project and program management, including portfolio management.

The most widely used publications of these in English are listed in the References at the end of this book and can be downloaded at the links given there under 1) Project Management Institute (PMI), 2) Project Management Association (UK), 3) United Kingdom Government, and (4) the International Standards Organization (ISO).

Project Portfolio Management Information System Applications

One of the greatest remaining challenges today for enterprises wanting to achieve the full benefits of effective project portfolio management is to adapt and implement a truly integrated and fully capable information system that provides the needed planning, scheduling, estimating, accounting, evaluating, reporting, and risk management information that is efficiently integrated with the corporate accounting and resource management information systems.

> "One of the greatest remaining challenges today is to adopt and implement a truly integrated and fully capable information system."

Some of the most widely used project portfolio management information systems include:

Advanced Management Solutions: Realtime Enterprise

CA Technologies

Compuware Changepoint

Dekker, Ltd: Dekker Trakker

Deltek Integrated Program Management,

HP Project and Portfolio Management Center

IBM Rational Software

Microsoft: MS Project and Project Server

Oracle Primavera P6 Enterprise Project Portfolio Management

Planview Enterprise Portfolio Management

SAP Portfolio and Project Management

Safran North America: Project Management Toolkit

Spider Project

The Need for One Integrated System

In larger organizations project management capability frequently develops independently in various parts or divisions of the enterprise over the years, creating islands of expertise, knowledge, and experience.

The best solution in the long term is to select one system that has all the capabilities needed both in the present as well as the foreseeable future.

Often these islands are using different project and program management information systems that have been developed internally or licensed from different providers. This creates a difficult integration problem when top management decides that a project portfolio management system is now required for the total corporation.

While it is technically possible in many cases to tie several different systems together at some level, the best solution in the long term is to select one system that has all the capabilities needed both in the present situation and within the foreseeable future of the organization.

This problem is especially acute within project-driven companies when several major customers demand that the company use a specific project management system to conform to the system that customer is using internally.

The lack of full system integration results in faulty decisions caused by conflicting, inaccurate, and out-of-date information, and it also results in un-needed expense and high error rates caused by multiple entries of information into the various separate systems.

The selection and implementation of one enterprise project portfolio information system in itself is a complex transformational project that requires the use of sound project management practices. The responsibility for such a project is usually given to a high level Project Management Office (PMO); the following chapter discusses PMOs in some detail.

Selection and implementation of project/program portfolio information systems is a complex project in and of itself.

The next chapter provides the executive reader with an understanding of the **need for providing an organizational home for the discipline of project management**, the Project Management Office, and also an understanding of the range of options that are currently found in practice regarding **the roles and responsibilities of such offices** in various business, industry, and governmental sectors.

5
Project Management Offices (PMOs)

> ***Establishing a home base*** *PMO for the project management function is required.*
>
> ***A wide variety of roles*** *& responsibilities exists for PMOs and their placement in the organization.*
>
> ***Major problems*** *have been encountered with improperly defined PMOs.*
>
> ***Impressive benefits*** *are obtained from establishing PMOs: Survey results of 554 organizations in North America and the European Union.*

One milestone marking the maturity of an organization in project management (see Chapter 8) is its establishment of a home (or homes) for the project management function — project management offices/PMOs — at appropriate levels reporting to appropriate senior executives.

The existence of such offices under a manager or director of project management is a significant indicator of where an organization stands regarding its capability and maturity in this important management discipline (Archibald 2003, pp.89-90 and 149-156.)

The term 'project office/PO' or 'central project office' is sometimes used for this project management office. It is recommended that the 'project office' title be used only to refer to a specific, individual project (or program) office that is the office of one project (or program) manager.

The project management office/PMO has distinctly broader and different responsibilities than an individual project office.

Project Office (PO) Versus
Project Management Office (PMO)

- **A PO is usually the home of a specific project or program; it is a temporary establishment created for a single project or program.**
- **A PMO is the home for the Project Management Function; it is a permanent establishment and knowledge base for continued development and application of Corporate Project Management skills and innovations.**
- **An established PMO is a significant indicator of corporate project management maturity.**

The Chief Projects Officer (CPO) Role

A number of organizations have appointed a Chief Projects Officer (CPO).[15] Usually this person will hold responsibility for the organization's Project Management Office. An Internet search on 'CPO' will yield a number of pertinent hits, including LinkedIn groups and blog sites devoted to this subject.

There is a similarity between the COO position for integrating and correlating an organization's on-going operations and the CPO position with similar responsibilities for the organization's projects. Steve Jobs was actually the CPO of Apple for his entire time there and propelled Apple to what it is today with his project direction.

---

[15] PM network. Vol. 24, no. 12 (Dec. 2010), p. [26]-31.

Implementation and Evolution of PMOs

The development of an effective project management office is normally an evolutionary process in most organizations. Knutson (1999) identifies three basic variations in the role of the project management office together with their primary responsibilities:

1. The PMO in a staff role:
    a. Keeper of the methodology.
    b. Mentoring/coaching.
    c. Librarian.
    d. Source of history.
    e. Prescreening of phase review reports.
2. The PMO in an Enterprise-Administrative Role; the above plus:
    a. Multi-project reporter.
    b. Priority-setting coordinator.
    c. Resource tracker.
    d. Administrator.
    e. Monitor.
    f. Change controller.
3. The PMO in a line role; all of the above plus:
    a. Manager of projects.
    b. Leader.

Alternative Charters for PMOs

Current project management literature describes a wide range of alternative charters for PMOs at various levels in an organization. A PMO can be designed to meet the needs of a total enterprise or corporation, a business unit, an operating division, a project portfolio, or a multi-project program.

The organizational scope and services to be performed for the organization by the PMO can vary widely as indicated by the following possible alternatives.

Range of potential PMO organizational scope:

- Corporate/enterprise-wide.
- Business Unit/Operating Division.
- Product Line.
- Project Portfolio.
- Multi-project Programs.
- Individual projects (replacing or overlapping with existing individual project offices).

Range of potential PMO responsibilities:

- Design, develop, implement, operate and continually improve the enterprise-wide project management system and its processes, systems and tools:
  - The project portfolio management process.
  - For each category of projects in the organization the project lifecycle management process/PLCMS and the software applications in support of the PLMCS and the enterprise-wide project management system.
- Acquire, disseminate and apply project management knowledge (the PM Center of Excellence):
  - Identify best PM and related practices within the organization's industrial, governmental, or other sector.
  - Capture, document, archive, retrieve and promulgate the organization's project management experiences, good and bad, within the organization for use with continual improvement efforts.
  - Disseminate this information throughout the organization in practical, useful ways to all affected persons.

    - Assure that the available information and knowledge is actually being applied appropriately within the organization.
- Provide project management training and indoctrination:
    - Design and deliver, in close cooperation with and through the appropriate training departments, the manager and specialist training and indoctrination needed to properly implement and use the organization's project management processes, systems and tools.
    - Evaluate and recommend the use of external training resources in project management as appropriate.
- Provide internal project management consulting and mentoring:
    - Conduct project risk assessments as requested using the most appropriate risk analysis and management approach for the situation.
    - Provide proposal assistance as required to assure that the project management aspects of proposals are adequately covered.
    - Provide facilitator/consulting assistance for project start-up planning workshops (see Archibald 2003, pp. 280-300.)
    - Conduct project performance audits of active projects as requested to identify opportunities for improvement and recommend corrective actions.
    - Provide on-the-job mentoring, training and consultation to program and project managers and to project specialists as required in all aspects of project management, including the operation and use of project management software applications.

- Develop and supply project managers and PM specialists:
  - Develop and oversee the administration of career paths in project management for project managers and project planning and control specialists.
  - Establish through the appropriate human resources departments effective performance and salary review procedures for project and program managers and project management specialists.
  - Establish assignments within the PMO that provide useful experience to project management specialists and unassigned or potential project managers in preparation for their assignment to positions with greater responsibilities.
- Provide direct support to individual projects or programs:
  - Provide administrative support to active program and project managers.
  - Provide specialist support to active project managers in risk management, project planning, resource estimating, project control, reporting, variance analysis, issue tracking, change control, contract administration, and other areas as required.
- Establish and operate a project control center with appropriate graphic displays and audio/visual aids and equipment for use in conducting project review meetings with each project team.

PMOs must evolve in responsibilities in most organizations as their PM maturity grows.

It is not recommended that an organization attempts to establish a PMO overnight with all of these potential responsibilities. Rather a logical evolutionary plan must be established that builds on the existing situation and in a series of steps or phases extends the PMO responsibilities as its success is demonstrated through its performance to date.

Problems and Pitfalls with PMOs

Failures of PMOs: Not every attempt at establishing a PMO has been successful over the years. In fact many PMOs have been established, flourished for a time, and then have disappeared.

The fundamental issue is one of centralization versus decentralization, coupled with the temptation that many practitioners have to 'build an empire.'

This issue can be addressed by looking at the range of responsibilities of a PMO that were listed earlier. Some of these, having to do with the overall processes, methods, systems and tools for the total organization, clearly should be centralized.

Others, primarily those dealing with planning and control of individual programs and projects and the reporting relationships of the several program and project managers, are not so clear-cut.

PMO Challenges:

- Centralization vs. Decentralization.
- Functional resistance and perceptions of loss of power and/or influence.
- Ownership and control of support services.
- Management oversight and authority of Project Managers.
- Temptation to "build an empire".

Project controls support should be controlled by each major project manager: One principle that is important to recognize is that the project planning and control support services provided to a major project or program manager should be directly controlled by that manager.

Especially on larger projects that required full-time support specialists, these persons should report directly to the project (or program) manager.

Attempts to centralize those support services and simply dish out the information to the various project managers usually are not very successful, for several reasons.

The detailed knowledge of the schedule, budget, expenditures, and related forecasts are the life blood of the project and vital to every project manager.

Having this information being produced entirely by an independent centralized staff that knows the problems it reveals even before the project manager is aware of them is not acceptable to an experienced project manager.

The result will often be that he or she will develop their own set of plans and schedules that they will use to manage the project, thus creating much duplication of effort and confusion in the various management reports that are being circulated.

Should project managers report to the PMO manager? The question of whether some or all project managers should report to the manager of project management in the PMO is also a difficult one.

If all major project managers so report this results in the manager of project management becoming an extremely powerful position—and therefore a likely target to be 'cut down to size' by political rivals in the organization.

Depending on the reporting level of the PMO and its organizational scope it may be much more effective to have the individual project managers report to various line executives. The manager of project management (or a PMO) can still exert their staff authority in the project management discipline over all of the project managers, but would not have day-to-day line authority over all projects.

Avoid building an empire: If the person given the job of manager of project management sees the assignment as an opportunity to build a PMO empire, and tries to capitalize on the interest in project management in that way, without considering all of the longer-term ramifications and respecting the position and authority of the involved program and projects managers, then the PMO will probably not last very long.

This will usually have a large impact to the organization since the need for the PMO may exist but the backlash from "remember we tried that" thinking can last well into the future. For that reason, the careful selection of the right PMO leader is as important as any other C-level personnel decision an organization makes.

Assuring Success of PMO Implementation

Recommendations for success: McMahon and Busse (2001) list these recommendations for assuring the success of a PMO implementation:

- **Place it at the top:** It is critical that the PMO be placed at the highest operational level or reporting to a steering committee at the highest operational level.
- **Build deep roots:** The importance of building coalitions, enterprise level placement of the PMO, and recurring staff education all contribute to building deep organizational roots that cannot be pulled out by a change in personnel, no matter the level.
- **Communicate:** Establish a communication plan to the entire organization regarding the benefits of a PMO.

Assuring Successful PMO Implementation:

- Place it at the top.
- Build deep roots.
- Communicate.
- Demonstrate value.
- Hold and disseminate results of lessons learned workshops.
- Build Project Management professionalism.

- **Demonstrate Value Added:** Implement easy to read reports distributed to the entire enterprise via company intranet or e-mail that describe successes and demonstrate the benefits of learning from failures.
- **Lessons Learned Sessions:** On completion of each project hold a lessons learned session open to all levels of participants, and build a knowledge management repository.
- **Build Project Manager Professionalism:** Treat the project manager role as a professional one, develop formal staff training, encourage professional affiliations and certification.

These authors list a number of other actions that will continue to build professionalism in project managers and the project specialist staff.

The State of the PMO 2012

The 2012 research report on PMOs, conducted by the PM consulting company PM Solutions (see references for the link to download their findings), is based on data from 554 respondents.

PMO Research Results:

- Most companies surveyed have a PMO.
- Definition of PMO Role is the greatest challenge.
- Increased PMO capability increases value provided thus reducing resistance.
- PMO staff members are highly experienced.
- More than half of those surveyed have standard training programs in place.

They represented organizations whose corporate headquarters were 70% in North America, 12% European Union, and the balance in countries across the rest of the world.

These organizations were from a very wide variety of industries and government and included a balance of small, medium and large companies with 10% from government agencies.

The PM Solutions 2012 report states, among many other findings, that:

- Most (87%) companies have a PMO (up from 40% in 2000), and 40% of those who don't plan to implement one in the coming year. The largest growth is in small firms: 73% now have PMOs compared to 48% in 2010.
- Formally defining the role of the PMO is their greatest challenge.
- The greater the capability of the PMO, the greater is the value that the PMO contributes to the firm. The value is no longer seriously questioned, although smaller firms are more likely to question the value.
- PMO staff members are highly experienced with an average of 10 years in PM; 40% are certified Project Management Professionals (PMPs) by PMI.
- More than 50% of PMOs have training programs in place. For executives who are responsible for the PM function within their organizations we recommend obtaining and reading this informative report.

The next chapter provides a summary of key topics related to managing individual projects that will **provide the executive reader with the general perspective** needed to give broad direction to the people who are managing at both the PMO and the individual project or program levels.

6
Managing Individual Projects

The core project management capability within any enterprise resides at the individual project level, and its effectiveness is a combination of two major factors:

- The project manager's authority, individual capability, knowledge, and project team leadership; and
- The 'project controls' capability in defining, planning, estimating, and controlling the project objectives, scope, cost, time schedule, risks, labor, and other required resources.

These two factors **depend on people who have different skills:** first, those needed as a project manager, and second, the project controls skills.

Although many successful project and program managers began their project management careers in the project controls area, they have had to develop different skills to become effective project managers.

Project success depends on *the Project Manager's authority and capability plus the Project Controls capability.*

The Project Controls function requires *the proper knowledge and use of advanced integrated PM information systems.*

The Success-Driven Project Management approach *is described as a typical example of effective project planning and control.*

Certainly a good project manager must understand and fully utilize the project controls capabilities within their organization, and the project controls function (which usually resides within a PMO) must understand that they fully support the project manager and are vital to achieving project success.

Project Management effectiveness depends upon:

- The Project Manager's authority, capability, knowledge, & leadership skills.
- The Project Controls capability to define, plan, estimate, and control the project objectives, scope, cost, schedule, risks, labor and other resources.

The Project Manager

For simplicity we will focus here on the project manager, recognizing that a traditional program manager will typically be directing two or more project managers and may also have broader responsibilities, as discussed in Chapter 2.

The manager or director of a major strategic enterprise transformational program will have even broader duties akin to those of a CEO for 'an enterprise within the enterprise'. Our discussion here will focus on a major project that requires a full-time project manager.

Project managers integrate the efforts of all project contributors (the project team) for their individual projects.

Project direction by the project manager to these team members consists of **what** must be done (scope of work), and **when** it must be done, with joint agreement with the responsible functional managers as to **how much** time, money and other resources will be required for each functional task.

This project direction is given through the responsible functional managers or functional team leaders assigned to the particular project. Functional managers give **functional direction** to their project team leaders consisting of **how** the work is to be done (technical discipline), **how well** it is to be done (quality and meeting specifications), and **who** will do the work on specific tasks or work packages (assignment of individual resources.)

Effective delineation and understanding of these principles is the key to making the project matrix organization a success.

The project manager responsibility can be defined in much greater detail with specific reference to the areas of planning, scheduling, negotiating, communicating, evaluating, leading, controlling, decision making and reporting.

Appendix A provides an example taken from a large multinational corporation of a typical project manager duties and responsibilities for a complex high-technology project under contract to an outside customer involving product design, manufacture, and field installation.

In practice such position descriptions must be tailored to the specific industry and project. Differences will occur for each category of project (for example, engineering/construction of capital facilities, product development, research, information systems, telecommunication systems, etc.), as well as for those differences caused by the nature of the parent organization and its national (or international) culture, the industry, and the projects themselves.

For detailed information about managing specific individual projects see Archibald 2003, Part II, Chapters 9 through 14.

Project Managers as Senior Executives

Many practitioners and authorities in project management have compared the integrative project manager role with the CEO and other executive roles, and postulate that experience as a project manager (especially on major transformational projects) is excellent preparation to become a CEO or other senior executive.

An extensive research project on this subject (Debourse and Archibald 2011) concluded that in project-driven companies (in which many CEOs have been project managers) those with experience as project managers are favored in their progression towards the senior executive position.

In project-dependent companies their progression is much harder since the project management discipline is not widely valued today within those companies.

Project Controls

Project planning and control involves two distinct areas: product and project. The functions required for each of these are:

- **Product** planning and control concern **what** will be the end results of the project:
    - Defining, designing and controlling the product characteristics;
    - Defining and controlling product configuration (change orders, etc.); and
    - Establishing specifications and controlling product quality.

- **Project** planning and control concern **how** the end results of the project will be achieved:
    - Defining and controlling project objectives & scope;
    - Systematically defining the deliverables and major elements of the project with indentured breakdowns (i. e. work breakdown structure/WBS);
    - Planning the work (tasks);
    - Scheduling the work;
    - Estimating the resources required (labor, money, materials, facilities);
    - Budgeting resources;
    - Assigning and authorizing the internal and external work and procurements;

- Evaluating and controlling progress (physical, cost, labor, schedule and cost control, technical;
- Planning and control risks.

For a detailed listing of the tools that are used for each of these important functions see Archibald (2003), pp 234-236. In addition to the several portfolio management information systems listed earlier in Chapter 4, there are many software tools available that are designed to handle these individual project controls functions.

As stated in Chapter 4, the continuing difficult challenge here is to enable the proper integration of all the information produced by these many product and project planning and control systems and tools.

The ongoing challenge of Project Controls is integration of information.

Success Driven Project Management/SDPM Methodology[16]

SDPM is briefly described here as a good example of integrated project controls methodology. It is based on a set of indicators measuring project performance and forecasting its final success, in addition to producing detailed planning, scheduling and control reports. The SDPM information system, which is fully supported by the Spider Project information system, supplies the project manager and project teams with the following information:

During the planning stage:

- Project target dates, costs and material requirements that could be achieved within the user defined probabilities of success;

---

[16] For more detail on this approach see Vladimir Liberzon and Russell D. Archibald, 2003; and Vladimir Liberzon and Victoria Shavyrina, 2013.

- Probabilities of achieving target project (and project phase) goals (scope, time, cost, and material requirements) – "success probabilities"; and
- Quantified time, cost and material contingency reserves or critical buffers that should be assigned to support achieving project goals with the necessary or desired probability.

During execution and control:

- Current probabilities of achieving various project goals,
- Success probability trends that are used for determining necessary corrective actions (it is worth mentioning that these trends depend not only on project performance but also on changes in project risk characteristics), and
- Current remaining contingency reserve quantities.

During project execution the project manager monitors and controls the current success probability and its trends. This trend information is the most useful for evaluating and estimating project performance and deciding if and what corrective action is necessary.

Trend information is the most useful for evaluating project performance and taking corrective action.

Need for Integrated Information: Effective project planning and control requires that the information regarding project scope, schedules, resources, finances *and related risks* be integrated at detailed and summary levels.

This requirement has been recognized for many years but it has not often been achieved in practice.

Effective project planning and control requires that the information be integrated at detailed and summary levels.

Integration Methods Used in SDPM: Integration of scope, schedule, financial and risk management for projects is achieved in the SDPM approach using these methods:

1. **Scope** is defined systematically using appropriate multiple breakdown structures that inter-relate all project information. The work scope or volume is estimated for each task, work package, or activity, together with the types of resources required and the planned rate of usage or resource productivity for each activity.
2. **Sequential, logical dependencies** of work and deliverables are defined using appropriate network planning methods.
3. **Resources** are:
    a) defined as consumable OR renewable; they can be utilized and produced on project activities;
    b) estimated as independent units, units in teams or crews, or interchangeable units within assignment pools;
    c) assigned to project activities;
    d) considered as constraints when their limits of availability are reached in calculating the project critical path, **in both forward and backward pass calculations.**
4. **Activity durations** are calculated, when appropriate, by combining work scope or volume with resource usage or productivity rates.
5. **Risks are calculated** by simulating risk events and using a range of three estimates where appropriate for 1) work scope and volume, 2) resource usage and productivity rates, 3) activity duration when estimated directly, and 4) calendar variation for weather and other factors, to produce predicted probabilities of success in meeting the desired target schedule dates and budgets.
6. **Project schedules** are produced in the usual manner by processing the network plans, but most importantly the true resource critical path is calculated to reflect logical

and all schedule constraints, including resources, in both the forward- and backward-pass calculations of the network plans. This has become known as the **resource critical path/RCP** to emphasize that resource constraints have been used in determining which activities are truly critical to project completion, and in the calculation of available float or allowable delay.

7. **Actual expenditures** of time, money, and resources are compared with plans, schedules and budgets to enable effective project monitoring and control, **including the use of earned value methods**.
8. **The current probabilities of success** in all areas (schedules, resources, financial) are calculated, and their trends are determined and presented graphically through analysis of frequently revised and retained project plans. Initially the desired targets for project dates, costs, and material or other resource requirements are calculated based on the desired probabilities set by the project manager and planner. When the target data are set, then the system calculates and the project planner evaluates the probability of their successful achievement.

Risk Simulation and Assessment in SDPM: Risk assessment can be accomplished in the SDPM approach using either Monte Carlo methods (many repetitions using random number generators) or using range estimates, usually three: optimistic, most likely, and pessimistic. The choice of which method to use in a specific situation depends on several factors.

Risk assessment can be accomplished in SDPM through either a Monte Carlo or Three-Point Estimate process.

Evaluating Success in Project Management[17]

Current project management standards show projects as consisting of four basic phases (Concept, Definition, Implementation, Handover and closeout), as shown in Figure 6.1.

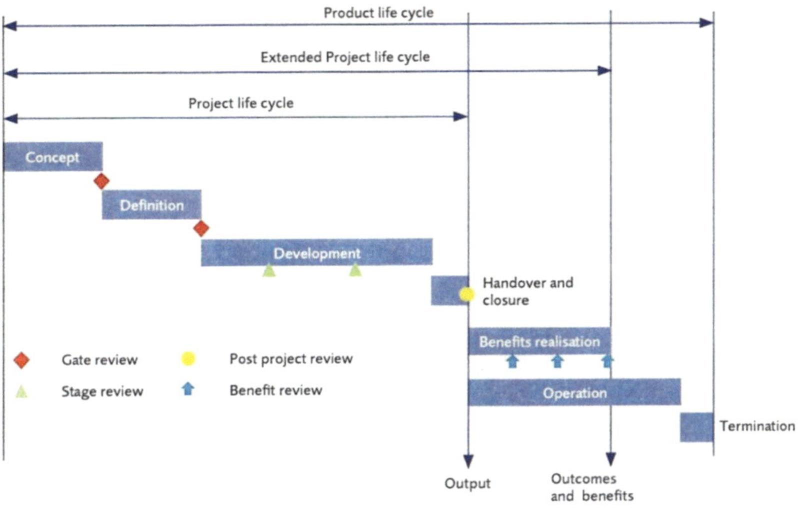

Figure 6.1. Standard project and extended life cycle model.
(Source: APM 2012 p 27. Used with permission.)

Following the Handover and Closure Phase shown in this and other standards there must be added a Post-Project Closeout Evaluation Phase for important projects, together with the Incubation/Feasibility Phase discussed earlier in Chapter 2. The Comprehensive Project Life Cycle Model that results from recognizing the existence of these two phases is shown in Figure 6.2.

---

[17] For a detailed discussion of this topic see "Archibald, I. Di Filippo, and D. Di Filippo, 2012.

Post-Project Closeout Evaluation Phase: After the project has been completed and its products or results have been delivered and placed in operation or use, its total success must be evaluated in four important dimensions to determine to what extent the business case objectives and benefits have been achieved, as described below.

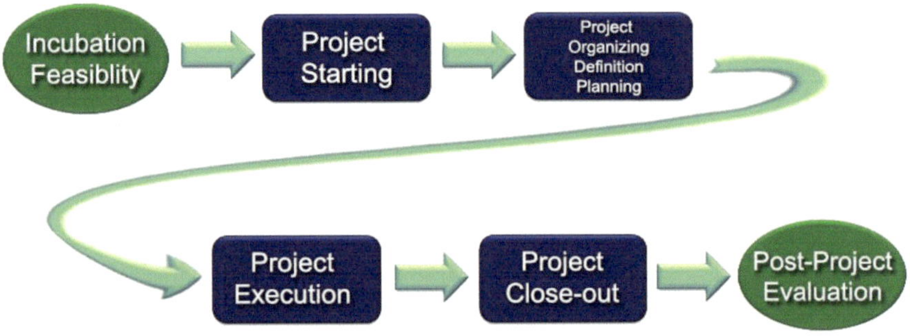

Figure 6.2. Six-phase comprehensive top-level project life cycle model.
(Source: Archibald, I. Di Filippo & D. Di Filippo, 2012.)

Dimensions for determining project success and value: The four main dimensions for measuring the overall project success are:

1. **Project Management Dimension:**
   - How closely did the project achieve the original objectives as defined in the Project Charter or Project Business Case?
   - Did the project meet the specified product specifications, and the approved budget, schedule, scope?
2. **Product-Business Objectives Dimension:**
   - How well does the product (including facilities, hardware, services, user and other documents, legal re-

quirements, and other important deliverables) meet the functional and business objectives that were used to establish the Project Charter and Business Case?

- How well does the product achieve its Key Performance Indicators/KPIs?
- What are the established Critical Success Factors (CSFs) and how well does the product measure up against these?
- Does the market buy, like and use the product? As examples:
- Does the public like the new motion picture that the project produced? Do they buy the number of tickets that were specified in the Project Business Case?
- Does the new chemical plant produce the specified products at the specified material and operating costs and comply with the established regulations?
- Do the users of the new IT system like and actually use the system, and achieve the specified benefits from using it?

3. **Stakeholder Satisfaction Dimension:** What level of satisfaction (accomplishment, enjoyment, pleasure, anger, conflict, frustration) exists in each of the project stakeholders:
   - The project manager, including their sense of perfecting their project management hard and soft skills;
   - Project core team members, including "Team Growth " in terms of self-efficacy and self-esteem in order to be able to count on a growing potential future (using the project to grow a team that is stronger and more efficient for the next project);
   - Functional contributors to the project and to its product;
   - Internal project executive sponsors;
   - External political and other sponsors;
   - Owners of the final product of the project;
   - Investors in the project and its product;

- Users and operators of the final product, including their:
  - enthusiastic appreciation of both the project and the product enabling them to perceive an even higher level of quality and differentiation, and
  - ability to perfect their skills in using the products of the project, thereby continually improving the original project results;
- Affected regulatory agencies;
- And others?

High project stakeholder satisfaction will enable the project organization to become the leader in its market. If the project manager and the team members are not satisfied, the project will lose effectiveness and efficiency and the project results will not be the best that they could have been.

Similarly, if the other key stakeholders are not well-satisfied the perceived success of both the project and the project results will be adversely affected.

4. **The Cognitive Team Performance Dimension:** Cognitive motivators and constraints have always had an important impact on team-working performance and the success of a project, as well as on the end results produced by the project.

   Only recently have these factors begun to be recognized in the project management community. The CSFs associated with this team performance dimension include how the project manager and the project team handle:

   - High decelerations or accelerations during the project.
   - Contingency factors that are hard to manage.
   - The Student Syndrome.
   - Parkinson's Law.
   - Overloading stress.

- Multi-tasking stress.
- Burnout Syndrome.
- Internal conflicts that can lead to crises.
- Drastic commitment reduction.
- Competence Borderline Syndrome (I'm going to do just what I have to do, no more!).
- ... and so on...

Achieving good success in this regard will have long-lasting impacts on all future projects and programs within the enterprise, as well as on the results of any specific project being evaluated. (Archibald & Di Filippo 2013.)

Dimensions of Evaluating Project Success and Value:
1. Project Management.
2. Project-Business Objectives.
3. Stakeholder Satisfaction.
4. Cognitive Team Performance.

Project Success and Project Value

Stanislaw Gasik[18] has introduced the concept that **project success is not the same as project value:**

"I currently think that there are two concepts: project success and project value. The concept of project value is wider than project success.... The concept of 'project success' should be related only to those goals which were precisely defined in the project charter or any other similar 'official' document.

The business goals achieved are the core project value, and everything which is gained outside of the initial (or officially changed during project execution) project goals should be added to the project value.

[18] Private correspondence, 2012.

So, for example, new relationships belong to the area of project value and not necessarily to the area of project success, although I can imagine a project which 'official' goal was developing of relationships."

We believe that the proposed four dimensions for post-project evaluation of projects will enable measurement of both the project success as well as the project value.

Project Success and Project Value:

- **Success** = Achieving business goals of the project with stakeholder satisfaction.
- **Value** = Those business goals plus additional unforeseen benefits.

Armed with the knowledge presented to the reader so far, executives will be in a position to ***place reasonable demands on their subordinates*** regarding their achievement of effective project portfolio management, as shown in the following Chapter 7.

7
What Executives Must Demand to Achieve Effective Project Management

Programs and projects exist in every enterprise of any reasonable size operating today. Therefore they are presently being managed in some fashion.

In large organizations there usually will be islands of strong PM capability. This often results in a sea of conflicting and overlapping PM practices and information systems.

Today, there is widespread knowledge of the state of the art of project management within many enterprises and government agencies.

As a result, senior executives of enterprises of all sizes can impose reasonable demands on their executives, managers and staffs to achieve excellence in the way their programs and projects are created, selected for funding, planned and executed.

These demands also include measurement of how well the

The understanding *presented in this book enables executives to make reasonable demands on their subordinates regarding project, program and portfolio management..*

31 specific demands *by CEOs and other senior executives are presented related to seven key areas of strategic and project management.*

When these demands have been satisfied *there will exist a very high probability that your organization will achieve excellence in leading and managing your innovative as well as your routine projects.*

ultimate benefits of the completed projects and programs have been achieved.

This Chapter 7 presents a list of 31 reasonable demands that CEOs and other senior executives can place on their staff and managers to assure excellence in the enterprise's project and program management capabilities.

Senior Executives must demand that:

Strategic Demands

1. Every authorized program and project clearly supports an approved **strategic objective** of the organization.
2. All significant **innovations** are achieved through application of the principles of project, program and portfolio management.
3. Each project's **risks** are identified, evaluated and managed using currently available methods and systems.
4. All projects are evaluated, prioritized and approved on the basis of the **same corporate criteria.**

Project Management Process Demands

5. The **program, project and portfolio management processes** of the organization are documented in a coherent, easily understood manner.
6. All projects are managed within their appropriate, defined **portfolios**.
7. The project management discipline and supporting systems are **fully integrated** with affected parts of the organization.
8. A network **enabled project management system** is selected and implemented at the most effective (project portfolio or total enterprise) level.

Roles and Responsibilities Demands

9. ***All*** of the project **integrative roles** are clearly defined, understood and assigned to qualified people.
10. A **portfolio steering group** is appointed for each project portfolio.
11. An **executive sponsor** is appointed for every major project and portfolio.
12. An experienced **manager of project management** is appointed for each PMO.
13. Appropriate homes (**PMOs**) are established within the organization for the project management discipline.

Manager Training and Authority Demands

14. All major project and program managers are given the **training** needed to ensure their effective performance.
15. Each project manager **respects the functional lines of authority** when giving project direction to their team members.
16. Functional (line) managers and project leaders **respect the project lines of authority** as exercised by the project managers.

Project Controls Demands

17. Every project is planned and controlled within the guidelines specified in the **corporate project management processes** documentation.
18. All project planning and control systems and procedures are **integrated** so that all project information is current and consistent throughout the organization.
19. Only **one summarizing project planning and control system** is used throughout the organization.
20. **Earned value** progress evaluation and forecasting methods are applied on all major projects.

21. The corporate project management process includes a detailed description of the **corporate project management information and control system.**
22. **All required technical, risk, and project information modules** are included in the corporate project management process and the overall corporate information and control system.
23. All (with specifically approved exceptions) **reporting documents** are produced by the supporting computer software systems.
24. The concepts of the **project/work breakdown structure (P/WBS)** and **project interface management** are applied to achieve an effective, sustainable level of detail in project documentation.

Project Team Demands

25. A **complete project team list** is produced and distributed to all key team members.
26. Each project team develops a **statement of project objectives** that all team members understand and support — consistent with the 'official' project objectives—within two weeks of the team formation.
27. Project teams set **both hard and soft criteria** for project success in the eyes of the key project stakeholders.
28. Each team establishes an **achievable project plan** to which all team members are committed.
29. The corporate project management process documentation includes the procedures needed to insure **effective teamwork**.
30. Project managers are given appropriate **leadership training** prior to their being put in charge of any major project.

Project Post-Completion Demand

31. A **post-completion appraisal** is performed on every project to 1) determine whether the business plan benefits of the project have been achieved, 2) document the lessons learned, and 3) improve the corporate project management process, practices and procedures.

Placing these demands on the executive's staff and managers communicates to the entire enterprise that top management understands what it takes to achieve the best performance possible in selecting and managing their projects and programs, and that top management fully supports the continuous improvement needed to assure the continued success of their enterprise.

Organizations need to measure their maturity in managing their specific categories of projects and programs, and benchmark themselves against their competitors. The following chapter describes how this can be done, and why it is important to be able to do so.

8
Maturity of Organizations in Project Management

Measuring the maturity of an enterprise regarding its project management success capabilities has become an important subject.

Hundreds of "Project Management Maturity Models" have been developed and used in the past two decades with the objective of measuring the level of project management maturity within all types of enterprises and for most of the many categories of projects.

These models range from simple to very complex.

The most widely used of these models have been developed primarily for large, complex organizations, and these have become excellent sources of business for specialized consultants.

The purposes of these models are to:

- identify where improvements are required,
- improve both the selection and the execution of the enterprise's programs and projects, and

The project management maturity of an organization *for specific types of projects can be measured effectively.*

PM maturity *can be viewed from three perspectives.*

This measurement is considerably useful *to determine where improvements are needed and to benchmark against competitors' capabilities.*

- benchmark one enterprise or one division of an enterprise against its competitors or counterparts with regard to the specific categories of programs and projects of importance to that enterprise.

Project Management Maturity Models:

- Identify where Project Management improvements are required.
- Enable benchmarking corporate PM performance against others, including competitors.
- Give clear indications of strengths and weaknesses.
- Can lead to significant competitive advantages if follow-up improvements are made.

Project Management Maturity Can Be Viewed from Three Perspectives

These three perspectives are:

1. **Operations versus project management:** How well the project management discipline is integrated with operations management. Indicators of relative maturity from this perspective can be subjectively determined by evaluating these factors, among others:
    a. Rank and responsibilities of Project Sponsors,
    b. PMO placements and definitions of their responsibilities, and
    c. Degree of conflict between Project and Functional Managers.

2. **Strategic enterprise management versus project and program portfolio management:** Are all projects within

the enterprise truly aligned with the current, approved strategic objectives? Are strategic transformational programs being managed as effectively as the commercial or delivery projects within the organization?

3. **PM Maturity of an *organizational unit* versus maturity within *project categories***: Many project management maturity models are applied (incorrectly, in our view) to measure the PM success capabilities of a company or division as a whole.

   They should be more appropriately applied to measure the organization's maturity with regard to each of the specific categories of projects that exist within the organization, as described in Chapter 3.

   An organization can be very mature and successful in selecting and managing a specific category of projects and programs, especially for commercial or delivery projects, but **at the same time it can be very immature in managing** its strategic transformational programs.

   As an example, a department can be very mature and successful in managing IT software projects while simultaneously being very immature and unsuccessful in managing the design and construction of a new office building or process plant.

Three Perspectives of Management Maturity:

1. Operational Management vs. Project / Program Management.
2. Strategic Enterprise Management vs. Project / Program Portfolio Management.
3. Maturity of an Organizational Unit vs. Maturity within a Project Category.

Importance of Measuring PM Capability Maturity

PM maturity measurement enables identifying the need for and opportunities to improve these capabilities within the organization and within each project category, and also enables worldwide comparison and bench-marking with similar organizations and project categories.

Research now supports the assumption that increasing an enterprise's PM maturity produces greater success in selecting, planning and executing its projects, and this in turn produces greater success of the enterprise. For example, five years of PM Maturity research in Brazil is documented at www.maturityresearch.com.

Research shows that increasing an enterprise's PM maturity produces greater success in selecting, planning and executing its projects, and this in turn produces greater success of the enterprise.

One interesting conclusion of this research is that **the existence for one year or more of a Project Management Office positively affects the organization's PM maturity level.**

The Prado PM Maturity Model, which is available on that site and shown in Figure 8.1, can be used without cost by any organization in the world that wants to determine how it stands against other similar organizations in several countries.

Unlike most PM maturity assessment processes, this model and its assessment process is easy to implement, requiring only 60-90 minutes to complete the questionnaire (depending on the size and complexity of the department or organization).

The core of the survey is a set of 40 questions to evaluate the maturity of a department within an organization. It is important that the questions are answered seriously and with honesty, and with consistent knowledge of the project management methods actually used in the department that is being evaluated.

This is a much faster and more cost effective approach than other PM maturity assessment processes. The results are provided on-line immediately upon completion of the questionnaire.

Through this process and the website it is possible to evaluate and benchmark the maturity in project management of private companies, not-for-profit and governmental organizations under direct or indirect administration.

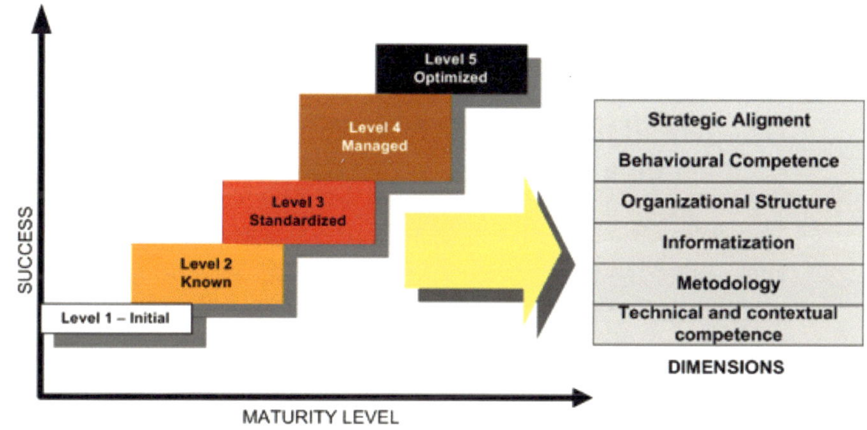

Figure 8.1. The Prado Project Management Maturity Model.

PM maturity in project-driven versus project-dependent enterprises: Project-driven enterprises (discussed in Chapter 2) typically have higher PM maturity levels than project-dependent organizations because the former's very existence depends of selecting the right projects and executing them effectively and efficiently.

Excellent project management is vital to the future of these project-driven enterprises. Research shows (see Debourse and Archibald 2011) that most CEOs of those enterprises have held project manager positions during their careers.

Project-dependent enterprises are often less mature in their project management capabilities because the importance of the

PM discipline is not widely recognized, and few of their CEOs or other senior executives have managed projects or programs during their careers.

We believe that every organization that has important projects under way will derive substantial benefits from initiating an effort to measure their project management maturity and determine where to initiate improvements in these important capabilities.

The discipline or profession of project management has experienced remarkable growth in its recognition and application throughout the world in the past three decades.

The following Chapter 9 of this book presents evidence of this widespread acceptance of the **need for and the use of these management principles and practices within all types of human enterprise.**

9
Development of the Profession of Project Management

Origins of Modern Project Management

The creation and management of programs and projects began to be recognized as a formalized management profession (or specialized discipline if you prefer) during World War II in the 1940s.

Its basic concepts first emerged within two important industries: facilities engineering and construction, and military/aerospace (Archibald and Villoria, 1967).

Project Management Associations, Standards and Certifications

A number of professional associations exist today that are focused on program and project management.

The largest of these are the **Project Management Institute (PMI)** (www.pmi.org), formed in the United States in 1969, and

The discipline *and profession of modern project management has evolved over the past 70 years.*

This profession *is now widely recognized as a vital capability within most types of organizations.*

Global professional associations *have developed useful PM certifications, standards and bodies of knowledge.*

Many universities *now offer Bachelor, Master, and Doctoral degrees in project management.*

the **International Project Management Association (IPMA)** (www.ipma.ch), formed initially in Europe as INTERNET in 1965, with its first conference in Prague in 1967.

Today PMI has 400,000 members in 120 countries and 266 formal chapters in over 80 countries, and IPMA has over 120,000 members in its federation of 55 national organizations around the world.

Both of these organizations have published extensive bodies of knowledge and standards in the field of project management.

PMI has distributed almost 4 million copies of the PMI Guide to the Project Management Body of Knowledge (PMBOK) in 11 languages. These two organizations have established certification programs for persons experienced in the project management discipline, and PMI reports that it has certified 495,000 people as Project Management Professionals (PMPs) worldwide.

There are also many other national and international associations devoted at least partially to project management that are not affiliated directly with PMI or IPMA.

The International Standards Organization (ISO) has published several standards relating to program and project management that are recognized around the world, including **ISO 21500, Guidance on Project Management,** a 44 page document published in 2012, which can be purchased at http://www.iso.org/iso/home/store/catalogue_tc/catalogue_detail.htm?csnumber=50003 .

The **Global Alliance for Project Performance Standards (GAPPS)** www.globalpmstandards.org has a competency based credentialing system for both project and program managers.

Many companies and governmental agencies also provide proprietary certifications in the project management field. As one leading example, the Office of Management and Budget (OMB) of the U.S. Federal Government initiated its **Federal Acquisition Certification for Program and Project Managers (FAC-P/PM)** in 2007 for all non-defense departments.

The NASA Academy of Program/Project and Engineering Leadership, at http://www.nasa.gov/offices/oce/appel/home/index.html provides extensive training and certification for its staff members. The U.S. Department of Defense of course has extensive regulations and certifications related to project and program management.

Many other governmental agencies and private corporations in a number of countries have published standards and have established academies and certification programs in program and project management.

Industrial Committee on Program Management (ICPM) of the National Defense Industrial Association (NDIA): Their Mission is "To provide a forum for senior executives of NDIA corporate member companies and senior Defense Department acquisition officials to meet periodically to review and discuss issues of common interest and concern.

"Topics for discussion will include program and acquisition management policies, procedures, best practices and issues which impact military systems development, procurement and use." http://www.ndia.org/Divisions/IndustrialWorkingGroups/IndustrialCommitteeForProgramManagement/Pages/default.aspx

College of Performance Management: An international, non-profit professional organization dedicated to the disciplines of project management and performance measurement. "We assist the earned value professional and project manager in professional growth and promote the application of earned value management. We are a growing body of professionals dedicated to managing projects on time and on budget." http://www.mycpm.org/

Construction Management Association of America: "The Construction Management Association of America is North America's only organization dedicated exclusively to the interests of professional Construction and Program Management.

"The Association was formed in 1982. Current membership is more than 10,000, including individual CM/PM practitioners, corporate members, and construction owners in both public and private sectors, along with academic and associate members. CMAA has 28 regional chapters and 43 student chapters at colleges and universities nationwide.

"The Mission of CMAA is to promote the profession of Construction Management and the use of qualified Construction Managers on capital projects and programs. CMAA is leading the growth and acceptance of construction management as a professional discipline that can add significant value to the entire construction process, from conception to ongoing operation." http://cmaanet.org/

The Association for the Advancement of Cost Engineering International (AACEi) is a leading-edge professional society for cost estimators, cost engineers, schedulers, project managers, and project control specialists. With over 7,000 members worldwide, it is industry independent, and has members in 80 countries and 80 local sections. AACEi provides a number of well-recognized certifications related to project management, as described at
http://www.aacei.org/certification/certExplained.shtml .

The Product Development & Management Association (PDMA) at www.pdma.org has 26 chapters in the USA and affiliates in 15 countries, and provides a Product Development Professional certification that is closely related to project management.

In addition to these, there are a number of other professional associations in engineering, construction, cost engineering, accounting, consulting, product development, and other fields that have developed standards and certifications related to program and project management.

University Degrees in Project Management

Numerous universities around the world now offer certificates and undergraduate and graduate degrees in program and project management. For example, to see a list of many university courses accredited by the PMI Global Accreditation Center in North and South America, Europe/Middle East/Africa, and Asia-Pacific:http://www.pmi.org/CareerDevelopment/Pages/Degree-Directory.aspx . The civil engineering departments of many universities offer degrees in construction management that are equivalent to other degrees in project management.

10
Summary:
What All Executives Need to Know

1. All Innovations are Achieved through Projects.

Therefore to manage innovation and change of any kind, the best project, program and portfolio management practices are required.

As we all know,

- Information is power.
- Knowledge is power.

The information in this book has given you a broad understanding and perspective of this relatively new management discipline called Project Management.

Armed with this information you are now in position to examine how the programs and projects within your enterprise – corporation, governmental agency, or not-for-profit association – are being conceived and managed.

***Book Summary** and quick reference guide*

1. *All innovations are achieved through projects*
2. *Project Management Concepts*
3. *Projects and Programs*
4. *Project Portfolio Management*
5. *Project Management Offices*
6. *Managing individual major projects*
7. *Demanding Excellence in Project Management*
8. *Maturity of Organizations in Project Management*
9. *Development of the Profession of Project Management*

You are now qualified to give excellent direction to your executives and managers to assure that your vital capability in this field of management – how you all manage innovation – is equal to or better than your competitors'.

2. Project Management Concepts

All executive teams – not just those directly involved in selecting and executing the many projects within their enterprise – must have sufficient knowledge about project management to carry out their daily responsibilities and contribute to the continual innovation that will keep the enterprise competitive and successful. We have provided the executive reader with what we believe to be a sound understanding of both the characteristics of projects and programs and of the principles and methods required to effectively manage them.

We have explained the important differences in:

- **Project management** compared to on-going **operations management,**
- **Transformational** compared to **delivery** projects, and
- **Project-driven** compared to **project-dependent** organizations.

The three basic concepts of project management are:

1. **Assignment of integrative roles** and responsibilities for projects at 6 levels in complex organizations.
2. **Application of integrated information** systems to plan and control each project, program, and project portfolio with all required elements of information through all their life cycle phases.
3. **Assigning, building, and directing each project team,** including all the human resources required to achieve the project's objectives.

The six levels of project management responsibilities are:

1. CEO.
2. Portfolio Steering Group.

3. Executive Project Sponsor.
4. PMO: Project Management Office.
5. Project Managers.
6. Functional Managers.

All project stakeholders:

- Must be identified early in the project and effectively involved in the project throughout its life cycle.
- Include all persons or agencies that are affected by or exert influence over the project and its results.
- Have a direct impact on both the success and ultimate value of the project.

The two primary objectives of project management are:

1. All projects are aligned with the organization's strategies.
2. Each project achieves its objectives and produces the desired value.

Project Management:

- **Uses** a structured approach.
- **Brings together** all skills and resources
- **Sets** objectives, scope, resources, schedule.
- **Delivers** intended results and value.

Origins of projects are different for:

- **Delivery** projects than for transformative projects.
- **Project-driven** than for project-dependent organizations.

After completion, a project must be evaluated to determine its success from the viewpoints of its:

- **Project management** (schedule, scope, cost, risks.)
- **Products** and other results.
- **Stakeholders.**
- **Team** performance.

3. Projects and Programs

There are many types of projects and many ways to categorize them for different purposes:

- Strategically.
- Operationally.
- Education and training.
- Career development.

One size project management does not fit all projects.

Major projects require:

- An Executive Project Sponsor.
- Application of the full set of project control tools.
- A full-time project manager.

Minor projects:

- Don't usually need an Executive Sponsor.
- Need application of less than a full set of project control tools.
- Can often be managed by a part-time project manager.

Strategic Transformational Projects:

- Are enterprises within an enterprise.
- Always produce significant innovation.
- Are always major projects or programs.

Mega Projects and Programs are:

- Enormous undertakings that usually involve consortiums of companies and governmental agencies.
- Beyond the scope of this book.

4. Project Portfolio Management

Project Portfolio Management:

- **Recognizes that all projects are investments** that must be governed, prioritized and managed using an established Project Portfolio Management process.
- **Is strategic** in nature.

- **Goes beyond** project and program management.
- **Encompasses** real world constraints and risks.
- **Provides major benefits** and strategic gains.

Three types of innovation investments are:
- **Empowering** to expand and grow.
- **Sustaining** to continue the existing business.
- **Efficiency** to reduce costs and improve efficiency.

"**Project portfolio management** can be a potent weapon to ensure an organization's investments work together and deliver true business results."

A coherent, documented **Project Portfolio Management Process and a Portfolio Steering Group** are vital requirements in today's globally competitive environment.

Good portfolio management will increase the number of projects completed on time & budget by 30%!

Project Portfolio Management is supported by a number of published guides, standards, and powerful information system applications.

The greatest information and control challenge continues to be the integration of project portfolio information systems with the well-established enterprise information systems.

5. Project Management Offices (PMOs)

A Project Management Office:
- **Is the organizational home** for the project management function.
- **Is the responsibility of the manager** or director of the project management function; this person may hold the title of Chief Projects Office (CPO.)
- **Usually evolves** in its responsibilities as the maturity of the organization in project management grows over time.

The challenges in establishing and evolving a PMO include:

- **How much centralization** of project support services is best for a particular organization.
- **Resistance** from the functional managers involved in projects.
- **Ownership** and control of project controls and support services.
- **Management oversight** and authority of project managers.
- **Temptation** to "build an empire."

There are a number of problems and pitfalls in successful PMO implementation, and a number of recommendations for assuring success have been provided.

A 2012 survey of 554 companies and agencies on three continents found that:

- 87% had a PMO.
- Defining the PMO role is the greatest challenge.
- Greater PMO capability brings greater payoff.
- PMO staff members had an average of 10 years of experience in project management; 40% are certified PMPs.
- More than 50% of PMOs have training programs in place.

6. Managing Individual Major Projects

Success of a major project depends upon:

- **Proper support** from the assigned Project Executive Sponsor.
- **The Project Manager's authority**, capability, knowledge, & leadership skills.
- **The Project Controls capability** to define, plan, estimate, and control the project objectives, scope, cost, schedule, risks, labor and other resources.
- **Functional Managers** respecting the Project Manager's project authority and the Project Manager respecting the Functional Managers' functional authority.

The Project Manager:

- **Integrates** the plans and efforts of all contributors to the project to achieve the objectives in the Project Charter.
- **Assures** that the interests of all project stakeholders are fully recognized and satisfied to the extent possible.
- **Provides project direction** to functional members of the project team: what, when, how much time and money is available.
- **Builds and leads** the Project Team.
- **Understands** and properly uses the Project Controls support capabilities provided by the organization.

The Functional Managers and Team Leaders:

- **Integrate the plans and efforts** of the project team members within each of their functions.
- **Provide functional direction** to assigned Project Team members: how the work is done to meet the specified schedule, how well it is done to meet technical specifications, who will do the work, how much time and money will be needed (for integrated planning purposes.)

Project Controls:

- **Support the Project and Functional Managers** with the skills and tools needed to define and control scope and to plan, schedule, budget, authorize, evaluate progress and risks, report progress and resources expenditures, and control the project through application and operation of integrated project information systems linked properly with the appropriate corporate information systems.
- **Include both project and product** planning and control information.
- **Require skilled specialists** to carry out its responsibilities and properly use the complex information systems required for major projects.

Integrated project management methodology requires the ability to:

- **Predict the probability** of achieving target schedules with available money and other resources.
- **Provide comparisons** of baseline schedules and budgets with current estimates that reflect progress and expenditures to date.
- **Effectively use earned value** methods.
- **Trend analysis** for key success factors.

Project success and value must be evaluated in four dimensions:

- **Project management:** scope, schedule and cost objectives.
- **Product and other results:** product quality and performance, documentation, operational and marketing objectives for the product, KPIs and CSFs.
- **Stakeholder satisfaction.**
- **Cognitive project team performance.**

7. Demanding Excellence in Project Management

Senior executives can now expect that their enterprise's project management capabilities fulfill the 31 demands listed in Chapter 7 for:

- Strategic management (4 demands)
- Project management processes (4 demands)
- Roles and responsibilities (5 demands)
- Management training and authority (3 demands)
- Project controls (8 demands)
- Project teams (6 demands)
- Project post-completion evaluation (1 demand)

8. Maturity of Organizations in Project Management

Measuring this maturity is important to:

- **Improve** the selection and execution of projects.
- **Identify** where improvements are required.
- **Benchmark** the organization against competitors for specific project categories.

Project management maturity can be viewed from three perspectives:

1. Operations versus project management.
2. Strategic enterprise management versus project portfolio management.
3. Maturity of the whole organization versus maturity in managing a specific project category.

One organization can be very mature for one project category and very immature in another category.

Project Management Maturity Models

- Identify where project management improvements are required.
- Enable benchmarking corporate PM performance against others, including competitors.
- Give clear indications of strengths and weaknesses.
- Can lead to significant competitive advantages if follow-up improvements are made.

Project-driven enterprises are very mature for the categories of projects they specialize in, but are not mature for other project categories.

Project-dependent enterprises must develop their maturity in specific project categories that are vital to their continuing innovation, growth and survival.

9. Development of the Profession of Project Management

The Profession of Project Management:

- Has grown rapidly in the past 20 years.
- Is supported world-wide by a number of professional associations.
- Has published bodies of knowledge and provides numerous certifications.
- Is recognized by numerous universities in many countries with advanced degree programs.

The Project Management Institute (PMI) today:

- 400,000 members in 120 countries.
- 200 formal chapters in over 80 countries.
- Distributed 4 million copies in 11 languages of the PMI Guide to the Project Management Body of Knowledge.
- 495,000 people as PMI certified Project Management Professionals/PMPs, plus other related certifications.
- Many related published standards.

The International Project Management Association (IPMA) today:

- 120,000 members.
- 55 national member organizations.
- Many published standards and guides in many languages.
- Robust multi-level certification process

The International Standards Organization (ISO) has issued ISO 21500, Guidance on Project Management, in 2012.

Other important project management related professional associations include:

- Global Alliance for Project Performance Standards (GAPPS).

- Industrial Committee on Program Management (ICPM) of the National Defense Industrial Association (NDIA).
- The Association for the Advancement of Cost Engineering International (AACEi).
- The Product Development & Management Association (PDMA).
- College of Performance Management.
- Construction Management Association of America.

Many other governmental agencies and private corporations in a number of countries have published standards and have established academies and certification programs in program and project management.

A large number of universities around the world now offer courses and degrees in project management.

Project Management Is Now a Vital Capability for All Enterprises Desiring to Innovate

It is clear that the discipline of program and project management is now an important area of specialization and in fact has become a management profession within the entire field of enterprise management. **Given the growing recognition that all significant innovation is achieved through projects, knowledge of and capability in project and program management has now become vital to all executives and managers in every sector of human endeavor.**

APPENDIX A
Project Manager Duties and Responsibilities

Example for a major High-Technology Design/Manufacture/Install Project Under Contract to an Outside Customer

Source: Archibald 2003, pp.207-2011

Project Start-Up

- Identify key project team members and define their responsibilities.
- Rapidly and efficiently plan and start up the project using project team planning start up workshops.

General

- Assure that all equipment, documents and services are properly delivered to the customer for acceptance and use within the contractual schedule and costs.
- Convey to all concerned departments (both internal and external) a full understanding of the customer requirements of the project.
- Participate with and lead the responsible managers and key tem members in developing overall project objectives, strategies, budgets and schedules.
- Plan for all necessary tasks to satisfy customer and management requirements and assure that they are properly and realistically scheduled, budgeted, provided for, monitored and reported.
- Identify promptly all deficiencies and deviations from the current plan.
- Assure that actions are initiated to correct deficiencies and deviations, and monitor execution of such actions.

- Assure that payments are received in accordance with the contractual terms.
- Maintain cognizance of all project contacts with the customer and assure that proper project team members participate in such contacts.
- Arbitrate and resolve conflicts and differences between functional departments on specific project tasks or activities.
- Maintain day-to-day liaison with all functional contributors to provide communication required to assure realization of commitments.
- Make or force required decisions at successively higher organizational levels to achieve project objectives, following agreed escalation procedures.
- Maintain communications with higher management regarding problem areas and project status.

Customer Relations: In close cooperation with the customer relations or marketing department:

- Receive from the customer all necessary technical, cost and scheduling information required for accomplishment of the project.
- Establish good working relationships with the customer on all levels: management, contracts, legal, accounts payable, systems engineering, design engineering, field sites and operations.
- Arrange and attend meetings with the customer (contractual, planning, engineering and operations).
- Receive and answer all technical and operational questions from the customer, with appropriate assistance from functional departments.

Contract Administration

- Identify any potential areas of exposure in existing or potential contracts and initiate appropriate action to alert higher management and eliminate such exposure.
- Prepare and send, or approve prior to sending by others, all correspondence on contractual matters.
- Coordinate the activities of the project contract administrator in regard to project matters.
- Prepare for and participate in contract negotiations.
- Identify all open contract commitments.
- Advise engineering, manufacturing, and field operations of contractual commitments and variations allowed.
- Prepare historical or position papers on any contractual or technical aspect of the project, for use in contract negotiations or litigation.

Project Planning, Control, Reporting, Evaluation, and Direction

- Perform, or supervise the performance of, all project planning, controlling, reporting, evaluation and direction functions (as commonly described in the project management literature), as appropriate to the scope of the assigned project.
- Conduct frequent, regular project evaluation and review meetings with key project team members to identify current and future problems and initiate actions for their resolution.
- Prepare and submit weekly or monthly progress reports to higher management, and to the customer if required.
- Supervise the project controller and his/her staff.

Marketing

- Maintain close liaison with marketing and utilize customer contacts to acquire all possible marketing intelligence for future business.

Engineering

- Insure that engineering fulfills its responsibilities for delivering, on schedule and within product cost estimates, the required drawings and specifications usable by manufacturing, purchasing and field operations, meeting the customer specifications.
- In cooperation with the engineering, drafting, and publications departments, define and establish schedules and budgets for all engineering and related tasks. After agreement, release funding allowables and monitor progress on each task in relation to the overall project.
- Act as the interface with the customer for these departments, with their assistance as required.
- Assure the control of product quality, configuration, and cost.
- Approve technical publications prior to release to the customer.
- Coordinate engineering support related to the project for manufacturing, installation, legal, and other departments.
- Participate (or delegate participation) as a voting member of the Engineering Change Control Board on matters affecting the project.

Manufacturing

- Insure that manufacturing fulfills its responsibilities for on-schedule delivery of all required equipment, meeting the engineering specifications within estimated manufacturing costs.
- Define contractual commitments to production control.
- Develop schedules to meet contractual commitments in the most economic fashion.
- Establish and release manufacturing and related resource and funding allowables.
- Approve and monitor production control schedules.
- Establish project priorities in manufacturing.
- Approve, prior to implementation, any product changes initiated by manufacturing.

- Approve packing and shipping instructions based on the type of transportation to be used and the schedule for delivery.

Purchasing and Subcontracting

- Insure that purchasing and subcontracting fulfill their responsibilities to obtain delivery of materials, equipment, documents, and services on schedule and within estimated cost for the project.
- Approve make-or-buy decisions for the project.
- Define contractual commitments to purchasing and subcontracting.
- Establish and release procurement funding allowables.
- Approve and monitor major purchase orders and subcontracts.
- Specify the planning, scheduling, and reporting requirements for major purchase orders and subcontracts.

Installation, Construction, Testing, and Other Field Operations

- Insure that installation and field operations fulfill their responsibilities for on-schedule delivery to the customer of materials, equipment, and documents within the cost estimates for the project.
- Define contractual commitments to installation and field operations.
- In cooperation with installation and field operations, define and establish schedules and budgets for all field work. After agreement, release funding allowables and monitor progress on each task in relation to the overall project.
- Coordinate all problems of performance and schedule with engineering, manufacturing, and purchasing and subcontracting.
- Except for customer contacts related to daily operating matters, act as the customer interface for installation and field operations departments.

Financial: In addition to the financial aspects of the project planning and control functions:

- Assist in the collection of accounts receivable related to the project.
- Approve prices of all change orders and proposals to the customer that affect the project.

Project Closeout

- Insure that all required steps are taken to present adequately all project deliverable items to the customer for acceptance, and that project activities are closed out in an efficient manner.
- Assure that the acceptance plan and schedule comply with the customer contractual requirements.
- Assist the legal, contract administration, and marketing or commercial departments in preparation of a closeout plan and required closeout data.
- Obtain and approve project closeout plans from each involved department.
- Monitor closeout activities, including disposition of surplus materials.
- Notify finance and functional departments of the completion of activities, tasks, and of the project.
- Monitor payment from the customer until all collections have been made.

REFERENCES

To download most of the references cited
in this book--arranged by chapter--go to
www.LeadingandManagingInnovation.com

APM, **Directing Change: A guide to governance of project management,** 2004. http://www.apm.org.uk/DirectingChange

Association for Project Management/APM, **APM Body of Knowledge**, 6th ed., 2012 http://www.apm.org.uk/knowledge

Archibald, Russell D., and Richard L. Villoria, **Network-Based Management Systems (PERT/CPM),** New York: John Wiley & Sons, 1967.

Archibald, Russell D., **Managing High-Technology Programs and Projects**, 3rd ed. New York: John Wiley & Sons, 2003.

___________, "What CEOs Must Demand to Compete and Collaborate in 2005: Unleashing the Power of Project Management in the Internet Age," 2002 Project Management Conference & Expo, Houston, TX USA, May 11, 2002. Available at http://russarchibald.com/recent-papers-presentations/strategic-enterprise/ceos-to-compete-coll-2005/

___________, "The Purposes and Methods of Practical Project Categorization," International Project/Program Management Workshop 5, ESC Lille - Lille Graduate School of Management , Lille, France. August 22 to 26, 2005, modified May 28 2007. Available at http://russarchibald.com/recent-papers-presentations/categorizing-projects/ .

___________, "A Global System for Categorizing Projects," **Project Perspectives 2013,** pp. 4-11, Vol. XXXV, International Project Management Association. Download at http://russarchibald.com/recent-papers-presentations/categorizing-projects/global-system-categorizing-proj/

also available at http://ipma.ch/resources/ipma-publications/project-perspectives/.

Archibald, Russell, Ivano Di Filippo, and Daniele Di Filippo, "The Six Phase Comprehensive Project Life Cycle Model Includes the Project Incubation-Feasibility Phase and the Post-Project Evaluation Phase," December 2012 issue of PM World Journal. Available at http://pmworldjournal.net/?article=the-six-phase-comprehensive-project-life-cycle-model-including-the-project-incubationfeasibility-phase-and-the-post-project-evaluation-phase-2 .

Butler, James, **Project** magazine, Nov/Dec 2010, p. 30, Association for Project Management, Buckinghamshire, UK. www.apm.org.uk .

Combe, Margaret W., and Gregory D. Githens, "Managing Popcorn Priorities: How Portfolios and Programs Align Projects With Strategies." *Proceedings of the PMI 1999 Seminars and Symposium,* Philadelphia, PA. Newtown Square, PA: Project Management Institute, October 10-16, 1999.

Crawford, Lynn, J. Brian Hobbs, and J. Rodney Turner, ***Project Categorization Systems: Aligning Capability with Strategy for Better Results***, Newtown Square, PA: Project Management Institute, 2001. ISBN 1-930699-3-87. 171 pp.

Debourse, Jean-Pierre, and Russell D. Archibald, **Project Managers as Senior Executives,** Newtown Square, PA: The Project Management Institute. 2011. https://www.pmi.org/Knowledge-Center/Research-Completed-Research/Project-Managers-as-Senior-Executives-Volume-I.aspx

Dye, Lowell D., and James S. Pennypacker, "Project Portfolio Managing and Managing Multiple Projects: Two Sides of the Same Coin?" *Proceedings of the 2000 PMI Seminars & Symposium,* Newtown Square, PA: Project Management Institute.

__________ Eds, **Project Portfolio Management – Selecting and Prioritizing Projects for Competitive Advantage.** 316 W. Barnard St., West Chester, PA: Center for Business Practices. 1999.

Fern, Edward, "Strategic Categorization of Projects," 2004. Available at
http://www.time-to-profit.com/TTPcategories.asp

Gladwell, Malcolm, "Creation Myth – Xerox PARC, Apple, and the truth about Innovation," The New Yorker Magazine, May 16, 2011. Download at
http://www.newyorker.com/reporting/2011/05/16/110516fa_fact_gladwell#ixzz28unWSiHkhttp://www.newyorker.com/services/referral?messageKey=901596c53f48c1c55c6d6844a897ee08

Global Alliance for Project Performance Standards (GAPPS) www.globalpmstandards.org

Hamel, Gary & C. K. Prahalad, "Strategic Intent," Harvard Business Review, May-June 1989.
ISO 21500 Guidance on Project Management, 2012, available at
http://www.iso.org/iso/home/store/catalogue_tc/catalogue_detail.htm?csnumber=50003 .

Knutson, Joan, "Project Office: An Evolutionary Implementation Plan," *Proceedings of the 30th Annual Project Management Institute 1999 Seminars & Symposium Oct. 10-16, 1999.* Newtown Square, PA: The Project Management Institute.

Liberzon, Vladimir, and Russell D. Archibald, "From Russia with Love: Truly Integrated Project Scope, Schedule, Resource and Risk Information," PMI World Congress – The Hague, May 24-26 2003. Available at http://russarchibald.com/recent-papers-presentations/integrated-pm-control/

Liberzon, Vladimir, and Victoria Shavyrino, "Methods and Tools of Success Driven Project Management," **Project Perspectives 2013**, pp. 32-37, Vol. XXXV, International Project Management Association. Available at http://ipma.ch/resources/ipma-publications/project-perspectives/

McMahon, Patricia, and Ellen Busse, "Surviving the Rise and Fall of a Project Management Office," Proceedings of the Project Management Institute Annual Seminars & Symposium, Nov. 1-10, 2001, Nashville, TN. Newtown Square, PA: The Project Management Institute.

NASA Academy of Program/Project and Engineering Leadership, http://www.nasa.gov/offices/oce/appel/home/index.html

Naughton, Ed., and Dr. Donnacha Kavanagh, "Innovation and Project Management," Institute Project Management Ireland, 2009. Available at http://www.projectmanagement.ie/images/assets/pdf/innovation.pdf

Pfeiffer, Peter, "Environmental Project Management in Brazilian Municipalities. Experiences of a Brazil-Germany Technical Cooperation Project", PMI GovSig Magazine, Oct. 2004, p 10.

PM Solutions, "The State of the PMO 2012." http://www.pmsolutions.com/insights/research/

PMI (available at http://www.pmi.org/PMBOK-Guide-and-Standards/Standards-Library-of-PMI-Global-Standards.aspx):

A. A Guide to the Project Management Body of Knowledge (PMBOK® Guide), 5th Ed, 2012.
B. **The Standard for Program Management,** 3rd Ed, 2013.
C. **The Standard for Portfolio Management,** 3rd Ed, 2013.

PMI **PM Network**. Vol. 24, no. 12 (Dec. 2010), p. [26]-31.

PMI "2012 Pulse of the Profession Portfolio Management Report," **PM Network**, June 2012, pp 14.

Prieto, Bob, **Strategic Program Management,** 2008. Construction Management Association of America, McLean, VA USA.

Prieto, Bob, "Systemic Innovation and the Role of Program Management as an Enabler in the Engineering & Construction Industry." ***PM World Today,*** February 2011 (Vol XIII, Issue II).

Ray, Michael, and Rochelle Myers, **Creativity in Business,** NY: Broadway Books, 1989.

Shenhar, Aaron J., James J. Renier, and R. Max Wideman, "Project Management: From Genesis to Content to Classification, INFORMS Conference, Washington, DC. May, 1996. Available at http://www.maxwideman.com/papers/genesis/background.htm .

Shenhar, Aaron J. and Dov Dvir, ***Reinventing Project Management: The Diamond Approach to Successful Growth and Innovation,*** Harvard Business School Press, 2007.

Shenhar, Aaron J., "What's the Next Generation of Project Management," *PMI Global Congress 2012 North America,* Session # RES01, Vancouver BC, Canada, October 20-23, 2012.

Taylor, John E. and Raymond Levitt, "Modeling Systemic Innovation in Design and Construction Networks," Center for Integrated Facility Engineering;, CIFE Technical Report # 163. Stanford University, October 2005.

Thiry, Michel, **Program Management,** Gower, 2010.

Tikkanen, Henrikki, Jaakko Kujala, and Karlos Artto, "The marketing strategy of a project-based firm: The Four Portfolios Framework," Industrial Marketing Management 36 (2007) 194–205.

United Kingdom Government, Best Management Portfolio available at http://webarchive.nationalarchives.gov.uk/20110822131357/http:/www.cabinetoffice.gov.uk/resource-library/best-management-practice-bmp-portfolio

- **Projects IN Controlled Environments (PRINCE2®)** – for project management
- **Managing Successful Programmes (MSP®)** – for programme management
- **Management of Risk (M_o_R®)** – for risk management
- **IT Service Management (ITIL®)** – for IT service management
- **Management of Portfolios (MoP™)** – for portfolio management
- **Management of Value (MoV™)** – for value management
- **Portfolio, Programme and Project Offices (P3O®)**
- **Portfolio, programme and project management maturity model (P3M3®)**

United States Government, **Federal Acquisition Certification for Program and Project Managers (FAC-P/PM),** http://www.fai.gov/drupal/certification/program-and-project-managers-fac-ppm

About the Authors

RUSSELL D. ARCHIBALD,
PhD (Hon), MSc-ME, BSc-ME
Founding Member & Fellow, PMI; PMP
Honorary Fellow, APM/IPMA
Chairman Emeritus, Archibald Associates llc

Globally recognized author, consultant and lecturer on project management with a career spanning more than 65 years, Russ has broad international experience in engineering, operations, program and project management as Management Consultant (Archibald Associates, Booz-Allen-Hamilton, CPM Systems, Inc.), Corporate Executive (Bendix, ITT), and Military/Aerospace (USAF Senior Pilot, Hughes Aircraft, Aerojet-General.) He has consulted to a wide variety of large and small organizations in many industries worldwide. Russ is a Fellow and Certified Project Management Professional (PMP) of the Project Management Institute (PMI®) (member No. 6, one of the five original founding trustees), an Honorary Fellow of the Association of Project Management (APM) in the UK, and is listed in Who's Who in the World (1985). He is the author of **Managing High Technology Programs and Projects** (3rd edition, Wiley 2003) (published in four languages), co-author of **Network Based Management Information Systems (PERT/CPM)** (1967), and author of 12 chapters in 9 books edited by others. Russ has presented 70 papers over the years at PMI, International Project Management Association (IPMA), and other conferences in North and South America, Europe and Asia, and is widely published in periodicals on professional project management. He holds Bachelor of Science (University of Missouri 1948) and Master of Science (University of Texas, Austin 1956) degrees in Mechanical Engineering. As a pioneer in the field, Russ received an honorary Ph.D. in strategy, program, and project management from the Ecole Superieure de Commerce de Lille (ESC-Lille), France in 2005, and received the **Jim O'Brien Lifetime Achievement Award** from the PMI College of Scheduling in 2006. Personal website: www.russarchibald.com, and he can be contacted at russell_archibald@yahoo.com.

SHANE C. ARCHIBALD, BSc
Managing Principal,
Archibald Associates llc

Archibald Associates is a consulting firm based in Washington State, USA, that specializes in project and program management and controls processes and systems.

Shane has 20 years of experience in the development and implementation of advanced, integrated project management processes and systems on large, complex projects and programs in several industries and governmental agencies. Most recently, he implemented the first phase of Project Controls applications and procedures for a large international heavy equipment design-manufacture-installation corporation, including advanced planning, scheduling, cost management, contract management, change management, and risk management processes. Previously Shane has:

- Developed and documented the project planning and control policies, processes and procedures for a US$10+ Billion transportation engineering & construction portfolio within one of the 50 United States, and managed the scheduling effort for that portfolio. Provided Subject Matter Expertise for a State-Wide Project Controls System Implementation.
- Managed the Project Controls Department for the Washington State Ferries, Terminal Engineering and Construction program, valued at US$1+ Billion.
- Managed the scheduling effort on a nation-wide US$4+ Billion telecommunication systems and facilities upgrade project.
- Managed the development process of a set of Web-based global enterprise products (shipping, pricing and logistics.)
- Implemented various project management and controls software applications and integration efforts, including several generations of Oracle Primavera systems.

Shane can be reached at Shane@ArchibaldAssociates.com
Also see ArchibaldAssociates.com .

Made in the USA
Las Vegas, NV
03 November 2026

57423758R00088